BOOKS BY LAURA INGALLS WILDER

Little House in the Big Woods
Little House on the Prairie
Farmer Boy
On the Banks of Plum Creek
By the Shores of Silver Lake
The Long Winter
Little Town on the Prairie
These Happy Golden Years
The First Four Years

On the Way Home:
The Diary of a Trip from South Dakota to Mansfield, Missouri, in 1894,
with Rose Wilder Lane.

West from Home:
Letters of Laura Ingalls Wilder, San Francisco, 1915.
Edited by Roger Lea MacBride, historical setting by Margot Patterson Doss.

The Laura Ingalls Wilder Songbook:
Favorite Songs from the "Little House" Books.
Compiled and edited by Eugenia Garson.

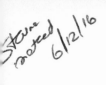

The Little House Cookbook

The Little House Cookbook

Frontier Foods from
Laura Ingalls Wilder's Classic Stories

BY

BARBARA M. WALKER

ILLUSTRATIONS BY GARTH WILLIAMS

HARPER & ROW, PUBLISHERS

NEW YORK

Cambridge		London
Hagerstown		Mexico City
Philadelphia		Sao Paolo
San Francisco	1817	Sydney

THE LITTLE HOUSE COOKBOOK

Text copyright © 1979 by Barbara Muhs Walker
Illustrations copyright © 1953, 1971 by Garth Williams

Library of Congress Cataloging in Publication Data
Walker, Barbara Muhs.
   The Little House cookbook.

   Bibliography: p.
   Includes index.
SUMMARY: Recipes based on the pioneer food written
about in the "Little House" books of Laura Ingalls
Wilder, along with quotes from the books and
descriptions of the food and cooking of pioneer times.
      1. Cookery, American—History—Juvenile literature.
2. Wilder, Laura Ingalls, 1867–1957—Juvenile
literature. [1. Cookery, American—History.
2. Wilder, Laura Ingalls, 1867–1957. 3. Frontier
and pioneer life] I. Title.
TX715.W1818 1979   641.5'9775   76-58733
ISBN 0-06-026418-7
ISBN 0-06-026419-5 lib. bdg.

FOR MY MOTHER,
MARIE NADING MUHS

Contents

Acknowledgments

LIKE THE LONELINESS OF PIONEERING, the loneliness of writing can induce illusions of self-sufficiency. Having reached a stopping point, I can pause, reflect, and, happily, disillusion myself.

It began when librarian Betsy Rush introduced us to Laura Ingalls Wilder's fiction and her real traces, and when the wedding of Bea and Bryan Peeke lured us west to South Dakota. Cheryl Peeke Edelen endured it all, from the first idea to the final manuscript.

Along the way friends became consultants; consultants became friends. Three authors who blazed some of the trails I traveled have been especially generous: Mariel Dewey of *12 Months Harvest;* Gertrude Harris of *Manna: Foods of the Frontier*; and Marjorie Kriedberg of *Food on the Frontier*. Marjorie's moral support and Mariel's Pilgrim goose and manuscript reading were special gifts. Through *The Everlasting Pleasure* Kathleen Ann Smallzried became as real as if I had known her, too.

Loans and leads came from Mary Allison, Patricia Allen, Helen Balgooyen, Anne Baren, Bill Bisharat, Caroll Boltin, Pamela Boyer, Sharon Cadwallader, Marilyn Chou, Mabel Techet Dean, June Dunbar, Nancy Dunnan, Carol Evenson, LaVerne Keettel Hull, Kathryn Kuhn, Sharon Moskow, Shirley Neitlich, Hilde Oldenburg, Ruth Rosenblatt, Elisabeth Williams, and Hallie Wolfe. Al Michel gave invaluable assistance with the index.

Approached in the line of duty, many people responded above and beyond the call: Kaye Anderson of the Saw Mill River Audubon Society, Warren Balgooyen of Teatown Lake Reservation, the late Isabel Callvert of *Gourmet* magazine, Barbara Feret, former librarian of the Culinary Institute of America, Craig Hibben of the Brooklyn Botanic Garden, Ordnance Park Corporation's president William E. Langbower, H. H. Lampman of the Wheat Flour Institute, Barbara Lane of Knudsen Dairies, Eleanor Lowenstein of Corner Book Shop, Y. Pomeranz of the U.S. Grain Marketing Research Center, Calvin Purvis of Amstar's Spreckels Sugar Division, Wayne Rasmussen of the U.S.D.A.'s Agricultural History Group, Richard Slavin III of the New York State Historical Association, Gil Thomson of the California Department of Fish and Game, archivist Alfred G. Trump of South Dakota State University and book dealer Elisabeth Woodburn. Longhorn breeder H. H. Hap Magee and Lieut. Harry Saglibene of the New York Department of Environmental Conservation were responsible for two memorable meals, 3,000 miles apart.

Testers are in a class by themselves. My California valentines are Sharon and Moira Inkelas and members of Los Gatos 4-H clubs led by Margaret Boone and Judy Smith: Mary Boone, Jane Fry, Christopher Jones, Ralph Jones, Sonya Jones, Tonya Jones, Susan Knox, Marcy Premer, Sharon Tesler, Rena Tesler and Terry Smith. New York tests were made by Pamela Clement, Peter Cooper, Linda Gilbert, Ellie VanHoogstraten, Jonathan Parsons and sporting staff members at Harper Junior Books.

Laura Wilder's memory lives not only in her fiction but through the work of memorial societies organized around her home sites. Because they are membership groups with much to offer Little House fans I have listed their officers below with mailing addresses. They have my thanks and admiration for their dedicated efforts and their courtesy to me.

Dorothy Smith, President
The Franklin County Historical and Museum Society
51 Milwaukee Street
Malone, New York 12953

Fern Marcks, Corresponding Secretary
Laura Ingalls Wilder Memorial Society, Inc.
Pepin, Wisconsin 54759

Mrs. Ralph Pearson, President
Mrs. John Clement, Founder
Little House on the Prairie, Inc.
Box 110
Independence, Kansas 67301

William Anderson
Laura Ingalls Wilder Memorial Society, Inc.
Box 344
DeSmet, South Dakota 57231

Irene V. Lichty, Director
Laura Ingalls Wilder Home and Museum
Mansfield, Missouri 65704

Book writers, even cookbook writers, must have a vision and underwriting
to keep them going. My daughter Anna, by her response to the Little House
books, provided the vision for the project and Edward, my husband, sustained us
through a very long gestation. Like Laura, they may have tired of frontier fare,
but they never complained. To them I owe the most.

Foreword

OUR FAMILY'S INVOLVEMENT with Laura and her food goes back to our first reading of *Little House in the Big Woods,* when I found myself making pancake men with my then four-year-old daughter Anna. Laura Ingalls Wilder's way of describing her pioneer childhood seemed to compel participation. Perhaps her native gift of observation and description was sharpened when she became the "eyes" for her blind sister Mary.

As time went by and Anna read and reread the series, we somehow acquired a coffee grinder in order to make "Long Winter" bread, we experimented with sour-dough starter, and we tried our hands at drying blackberries. From other mothers I learned that our impulses were far from unique. One mother even advised me to "skip *Farmer Boy* if you don't want to get into that ice cream making mess." In fact, we skipped nothing.

If the results were not always rewarding, the process was, and that is partly the reason for this book. Cooking was for Laura Ingalls a social experience and an apprenticeship. By cooking with her elders she learned something about food, something about work, and something about human communion. Cooking remains one of the few essential household activities that adults and children or older and younger children can share in modern urban life. This book is a gesture of sharing.

We hope it will be used by people working together. Cooking for Laura was often pleasurable, but it was never busywork or child's play. Her food was too hard to come by.

Eventually I began looking for authentic recipes for dishes merely sketched or mentioned in the "Little House" books. The search led to other writings of Laura Wilder, her daughter Rose, and their biographers, then on to sources of the period—pioneer diaries, local recipe collections, and cookbooks by professional authors. Always I have worked from the assumption that even in the fanciful *Farmer Boy* the details that illumine the fictional story line are true. The recipes in this collection use as points of departure quotations from Harper & Row's uniform edition of the "Little House" books.

Because food materials and kitchen equipment have changed so much since Laura's childhood, the finished recipes naturally involve compromises. I've transposed some of Ma's fireplace cookery to the stove and introduced precise measurements for all ingredients as well as twentieth-century temperature measurements (not without a sigh over the loss that has occurred in our sensory powers).

I have tried to remain faithful to an era that had neither baking powder nor the process of pasteurization. I have steadfastly refused to spike the sour-dough starter with modern dry yeast. Yet I have easily conceded to using store-bought trout and strawberries. These are clearly biases at work, and readers will find others, along with the inevitable anachronisms. I hope they will take time to inform me of my lapses.

Not all dishes included here will be greeted with enthusiasm at the table; some are admittedly historic, rather than taste, sensations. But all are revealing in one way or another. Taken together they turn out to be a wonderful way to rediscover basic connections, links that are often obscured in the complex modern world. By this I mean connections among the food on the table, the grain in the field, and the cow in the pasture. Between the food on the table and the sweat of someone's brow. Between the winter and dried apples, the summer and tomatoes, the autumn and fresh sausage. Between the labors of the pioneers and the abundance we enjoy today. Between children and their elders. Between the preparation of a meal and the experience of love.

B. M. W.

The Little House Cookbook

Chapter
1

Food in the Little Houses

LAURA INGALLS WILDER was born in Pepin, Wisconsin, in 1867. In 1932, when she was sixty-five years old, she wrote her first book, *Little House in the Big Woods,* a lightly fictionalized account of her childhood days in her first frontier home. The next year she followed with *Farmer Boy,* recounting her husband Almanzo's boyhood on the prosperous Wilder dairy farm outside Malone, New York, not far from the Canadian border. During the next ten years she wrote and published the seven books that have, with the first two, become known around the world (and in fifteen languages) as the "Little House" books—*Little House on the Prairie, On the Banks of Plum Creek, By the Shores of Silver Lake, The Long Winter, Little Town on the Prairie, These Happy Golden Years,* and *The First Four Years.* In them she traced the migration of her family—Ma, Pa, and sisters Mary, Grace, and Carrie—from Pepin to the southern Kansas border, on to Walnut Grove, Minnesota, to Silver Lake, South Dakota, and finally to De-Smet, South Dakota. *These Happy Golden Years* is set on the Homestead Act claim settled by the Ingallses outside DeSmet; it ends with Laura's marriage at eighteen to Almanzo Wilder. *The First Four Years* tells of their life together on their own claim not far away.

Throughout this now classic series much of the action centers on food—hunting it, growing it, losing it to natural disasters, cooking it, preserving it, and eating it. On the frontier, feeding the family was a task that took most of everyone's time.

For Pa there was no weekly paycheck to be exchanged for shelter, clothing, and groceries. Pa pursued the food with gun, trap, and plow; Ma prepared and preserved it; and the children helped in both activities.

Food also looms large in this pioneer chronicle because there was rarely enough of it. Though she tells of being listless and weak from near-starvation during the Long Winter, the storybook Laura never complains of hunger. Yet the real grownup Laura's memory for daily fare and holiday feasts says more about her eagerness for meals, her longing for enough to eat, than it does about her interest in cooking. *Farmer Boy* is not merely her husband's story; it is her own fantasy of blissful youth, surrounded on all sides by food.

The Wilders were established farmers in an area that favored dairy herds and offered a market for dairy products. Caroline Quiner and Charles Ingalls—Ma and Pa—had been raised as farmers, but on land newly turned to the plow. Ma and Pa would carry on the pioneer tradition of their parents, struggling to establish a farm with cash crops, products to sell, but living meanwhile as nomads, off staples from the country store and food from the wilds.

It was their migrant life, as much as the seasons, that shaped the Ingallses' diet, and this fact provides the organizing principle of our recipes. Basic to their lives were the tools and staples that could be paid or bartered for, regardless of place or season. Next in importance were the gifts of Nature—fish from the rivers, berries from the brush, game from the woods and prairies—to be gathered in the summer and fall and preserved for winter and spring. Bread from their own wheat was the Ingallses' dream; usually it was made from store flour. Fresh garden vegetables and barnyard meats and eggs and cheeses were, for both Laura and Almanzo, childhood fare that became elusive prizes.

Neither Mother Wilder nor Ma knew anything of the science of nutrition; vitamins and vitamin deficiencies are discoveries of the twentieth century. But they knew that a diet varied enough to please the palate and eye was likely to be a healthful one as well. Picture, if you will, this Sunday dinner on the Wilder farm:

[Almanzo] felt a little better when he sat down to the good Sunday dinner. Mother sliced the hot rye'n'injun bread on the bread-board by her plate. Father's spoon cut deep into the chicken-pie; he scooped out big pieces of thick crust and turned up their fluffy yellow under-sides on the plate. He poured gravy over them; he dipped up big pieces of tender chicken, dark meat and white meat sliding from the bones. He added a mound of baked beans and topped it with a quivering slice of fat pork. At the edge of the plate he piled dark-red beet pickles. And he handed the plate to Almanzo.

Silently Almanzo ate it all. Then he ate a piece of pumpkin pie, and he felt very full inside. But he ate a piece of apple pie with cheese.

If this seems heavy with starches and sweets, remember that it was served to a family accustomed to hard physical labor and unaccustomed to centrally-heated houses. And that it was described by an author who ate far more cornmeal, lean game and wild fruits as a child than breads, fats, and desserts. A special meal on the prairie—the one for Mr. Edwards, for instance, consisted of "stewed jack rabbit with white-flour dumplings and plenty of gravy . . . steaming-hot cornbread flavored with bacon fat . . . molasses to eat on the cornbread" and coffee sweetened with brown sugar.

Celebrations and social gatherings were a time for eating. Socializing for young and old took the form of church suppers and evenings at home popping corn or pulling candy. But the reverse was not always true; mealtimes were not a time for socializing. Usually children were permitted to speak only when spoken to. Both Almanzo and the Ingalls girls were fortunate in having parents who conversed at the table and included them. Certainly they were better off than many colonial children, a century earlier, who stood by as their parents occupied the only chairs at the table and waited for morsels from grownups' plates.

As the Ingallses moved westward into more primitive conditions, the eastern United States was in the throes of the Industrial Revolution. The Great Centennial Exhibition of 1876 was virtually a preview of the twentieth century. Visitors to its vast Philadelphia site could see Alexander Graham Bell and his new telephone, observe a demonstration "kindergarten," and hear Joseph Lister expound his latest discoveries about disinfecting wounds. They could dine on the most cosmopolitan fare in restaurants featuring French, German, Austrian, and Chinese dishes.

That same year, 1876, the storybook Laura was eight (nine in real life) and living "on the banks of Plum Creek." Her family had just moved from the Kansas prairie, where the cooking was done, as it had been done for centuries, in an open fireplace. Her new home had a wonderful surprise for Ma, an iron cookstove. More up-to-date than the Wisconsin stove, it had a "big door on the side" which opened to show a "big square place with a shelf across it"; in other words, an oven.

In experiencing both hearth cooking and stove cooking, Laura witnessed the greatest change in the whole history of home cookery. She would live to see many more changes—to kerosene and coal stoves, to gas and electric stoves, and to automatic coffee pots and electric dishwashers—and she would never lose her sense of wonder about them. On a visit to her daughter in San Francisco in her forty-eighth year, she wrote to Almanzo, "Aladdin with his wonderful lamp had no more power than the modern woman in her kitchen. . . ."

The Cook's Domain

THE FIRST KITCHEN Laura Ingalls Wilder describes in her stories is her grandmother's. To a five-year-old raised in a one-room cabin that functioned as a sitting room, dining room, kitchen, bedroom, and workshop, a room just for cooking seemed quite grand indeed!

It was not exactly what we would call a kitchen. There were no water taps and sink, only pails and basins for carrying and heating water from the outdoor pump. There was no refrigerator or icebox. Iceboxes had been invented, but they needed block ice for cooling. Only prosperous farmers like the Wilders had the pond, the horse-drawn saw, the team, and the icehouse needed for harvesting block ice.

As for food, it was stored mostly elsewhere. Potatoes, turnips, beets, and apples were in the cellar. Below the frostline and far from the sun, the cellar kept produce cool without danger of drying or freezing. Hams, pumpkins, squashes, onions, and dried peppers hung in the attic, where it was also cool in winter, but dry and sometimes smoky from the fireplace below. Fresh meat, if stored at all, was in a "natural" freezer—a shed outside the main entrance to the house that also worked as a storm door, kept the firewood dry, and had shelves for meat from autumn hunting and butchering.

Even the cooking pans and utensils, the dishes and dry stores —flour, cornmeal, salt—had a place of their own, the pantry. In

some houses this was a room in itself; in others it was little more than a set of shelves. Unheated as well as covered (with a door or cloth) against wood ash and flies, it usually also held the week's baking and the day's milk.

What made Grandma's room a kitchen, and a modern one at that, was the cookstove. It was called that to distinguish it from stoves used to heat rooms. It had been invented around the time Ma Ingalls was born, by an American living in Europe. It was made of iron and decorated with fancy scrolls.

This stove heated cooking pots and pans, either on a counter surface with holes called burners or in an oven. There were no dials and buttons; you regulated the temperature by the amount and kind of wood you burned—seasoned ash, oak, and walnut for a bright fire; gray birch, poplar, or green hardwood for a slow one. On

baking day you knew the oven was ready for bread when you could
keep your bare hand in it to the count of twenty and no longer.

Wonderful as they were for cooking hasty pudding and
pumpkin and for baking pies, the stoves were slow in replacing all
fireplace cookery. For as long as fireplaces were used to heat houses
they were the preferred place for cooking meat. Roasting, it was
called, and it was done by turning the meat on a spit near live coals.
Cookbooks of the day gave advice on both spit and oven roasting,
including how to avoid a "stovey" taste. To this day "charcoal-
broiled" meats have a special appeal.

Ma Ingalls had a cookstove in the Wisconsin house, but it was
back to open-fire cookery for her when the family crossed the frozen
Mississippi and headed for Kansas. Throughout the journey and the
year in the prairie house, Ma would do with the few utensils she was
able to pack, beginning with the all-important iron bake-oven and
spider. Laura Wilder tells just how they were used:

> *[Ma] set the iron bake-oven in the coals. . . . While it heated she
> mixed cornmeal and salt with water and patted it into little cakes. She
> greased the bake-oven with a pork-rind, laid the cornmeal cakes in it,
> and put on its iron cover. Then Pa raked more coals over the cover,
> while Ma sliced fat salt pork. She fried the slices in the iron spider. If
> it had had no legs, it would have been only a frying pan.*

A teakettle of iron or heavy copper and possibly a saucepan completed the heavy cookware. There was a tin kitchen for spit roasting,
and also of tin, a coffeepot, a dripping pan for catching meat juices,
and plates and cups for the table. With hope of a milk cow there
must also be milk pans for settling the new milk—shallow round
tins, like our layer-cake pans, in which the cream could rise to a thick
sheet. Square baking pans or flat tin sheets held bread, cookies, or
biscuits.

The coffee grinder went along in the wagon, as well as the
crescent-shaped chopping tool and the wooden bowl that cradled
it. So probably did a board for working bread and pastry dough and
a mixing bowl.

A popular cookbook from 1884, the year of Laura's marriage,
lists one hundred "utensils with which a kitchen should be fur-

nished." Included are a fish kettle, a lemon squeezer, a jagging iron, a melon mold, and the latest convenience, the Dover egg beater. Even on the claim, when she at last had a real kitchen—"so spacious now, with only the stove, the cupboard, the table and chairs in it" —Ma Ingalls probably had few of these specialized tools. As for Mother Wilder's utensil stock, we can only wonder. The very fact of the tin-peddler's visit suggests that her kitchen was well equipped. On one occasion, we know, she traded rags for "milk-pans and pails, the colander and skimmer, and the three baking pans." Obviously her taste did not run to rotary egg beaters, ice cream freezers, and other conveniences that might soften the children's muscles.

For pioneer housewives with no butchers, bakers, or candle-makers to serve them, the work of preparing meals was enormous. The farmer might butcher steer or pig, clean and scale the fish, and skin the game, but it was the cook who dressed the meat and plucked the fowl. The kitchen garden was hers to plant and tend. She shared in the milking, skimmed the milk, scalded the utensils, and churned the butter.

Every day water had to be brought from the well for washing food and dishes; pots had to be scoured with sand; slicing, dicing, and beating had to be done without mechanical aids. Water had to be heated for laundry, linens and clothes scrubbed, hung to dry, and ironed by hand. The fire, whether on hearth or stove, always had to be tended with an eye to the day's cooking needs as well as comfort. Even with children to help, the housewife needed a strong back and a quick mind. In organizing her work, traditions like this one helped her:

> *Wash on Monday*
> *Iron on Tuesday*
> *Mend on Wednesday*
> *Churn on Thursday*
> *Clean on Friday*
> *Bake on Saturday*
> *Rest on Sunday.*

If you followed this plan, your house would be clean for Sunday sitting, with or without guests; your butter and baked goods would be fresh for Sunday dinner; and your best clothes and linens would be washed before any stains could set.

All these things a woman learned early in life by assisting her mother. At least that was so on the frontier; in more settled parts of the expanding country, girls and boys spent their days in school, learning from books. A growing number of young women were becoming the audience for another growing group, the writers of housekeeping manuals and "receipt" books. These industrious authors deplored a society in which prospective housewives learned Latin and literature at the expense of cooking and sewing, and they rushed to fill the void with advice on everything from hiring servants and curing croup to buying kerosene and making ink. One of the most popular was Eliza Leslie's *Directions for Cookery,* which went through thirty-eight editions before the author's death in 1858. It is still available today.

Women at home found escape as well as instruction in ladies' magazines offering food and fashion news and romantic stories in serial form. By the time Laura was a mother, the venerable *Peterson's Magazine* and *Godey's Lady's Book* had competition from *Harper's Bazaar, Good Housekeeping,* and *Ladies' Home Journal.*

There was even a strong movement spreading westward to give recognition to housekeeping as a profession requiring scientific training. Catharine Beecher, with help from her sister Harriet Beecher Stowe, not only wrote outstanding housekeeping manuals but also founded schools where women studied domestic arts along with academic subjects. In the decades that followed the Civil War, commercial cooking schools flourished in Philadelphia, New York, and Boston. Land grant colleges in Iowa, Kansas, and Illinois began offering courses for women that developed, before the century had ended, into full-fledged colleges of home economics.

Laura Ingalls Wilder would catch up with all these developments and even contribute to the literature of homemaking, but long after her own skills had been honed on the grindstone of lonely experience. From teachers sometimes wise and sometimes foolish, but never remote, she learned enough to qualify as a teacher and wage earner herself. From her remarkable mother she learned the skills she would need for the inevitable responsibilities of managing a farm home. When economics and romance conspired to make her at eighteen the mistress of her own farm, she was unseasoned and unsure but competent. She managed well enough to become comfortable and to undertake, late in life, a new career as a writer of books. We can't help but admire her and be grateful.

Staples from the Country Store

"SELF-SUFFICIENCY" was the badge of the American pioneer. Self-sufficient, indeed, the Ingallses seemed. Yet they never dared settle too far from the country store. It was their lifeline, supplying the essentials that made survival possible and the luxuries that made life livable.

Before there could be a house, garden, clothing, and game-food in the pot, there must be an ax, nails, a scythe, a plow, needles, thread, cloth, a gun, powder, and a pot. All these could be had at the general store, that peculiarly American combination of goods and services that flourished in the horse-and-wagon days. What's more, when cash was low, they could be had on credit or in exchange for pelts, produce, or labor. Even ashes (for making lye) and rags (for papermaking) were taken in trade.

Basic foods like cornmeal, the Ingallses' mainstay on the prairie, came from the store. As Ma told Pa, "You could find a bee-tree, but there's no cornmeal tree to be found, so far as I know, and we'll raise no corn till next year." Even a corn crop was useless without a mill nearby.

Dried beans were often bought between crops, along with the molasses that transformed them into a favorite dish. Molasses came in barrels from sugar cane plantations in the South; the residue of the refining process, it was the cheapest sweetener available. Brown sugar was next in price. White sugar, requiring the most processing, was the most expensive. Even when maple sugar was plentiful, it was nice to have white sugar that didn't cloud tea or overwhelm delicate flavors.

"It seems strange to have everything one could want to work with," Ma said at the end of the long winter when the supply train finally arrived. "Now I have cream of tartar and plenty of saleratus, I shall make a cake."

She was speaking of two important stores that made the difference between heavy baked goods and light ones. Saleratus, now called baking soda, and cream of tartar are the main components of baking powder, a key ingredient of cakes and quickbreads.

Teas from China and India; coffee beans from Ceylon and South America; peppercorns, mace, nutmeg, and cinnamon from Malay; ginger from Africa and the West Indies, salt from American mines—these were the extras that made food into meals and eating a pleasure as well as a necessity. Stored in barrels, piggins, noggins, firkins, and tierces, they were scooped out and sold by weight for home brewing and grinding. These imported luxuries were referred to as "groceries." The more commonplace stores, also shipped long distances, like flour, salt pork, dried fruits, and vegetables, were the "produce" of the day. Anything that did not have to be weighed or poured, such as an ax or a pail or a pencil, came under the heading "dry goods." Mechanical refrigeration was still in the future and, with it, fresh meat, milk, and perishable fruits and vegetables.

The general store also had some canned foods. The nineteenth century was the era of the can, beginning as it did with Napoleon's award to the chef who invented this way of preserving food for his troops. By Laura's birthdate, 1867, there were canneries as far west as Chicago and Wisconsin. To midwestern farmers the coastal canneries were most important, shipping delicacies they might otherwise never taste—shrimp from Louisiana, oysters and sardines from New England.

There were few boxed goods on the shelves; packaged goods grew up with Laura. Saleratus and later baking powder came in tins. But there were bottles of all shapes and sizes and colors containing "patent" medicines. From Burdock Bitters to Sands Sarsaparilla and Dr. Williams' Pink Pills for Pale People, each claimed unique cures for all manner of human and animal ailments. In fact, they were merely registered by name and not really patented, for that public action would have revealed most recipes to be more alcoholic than wine or beer. We know of only one Ingalls purchase from such stores, quinine. This was the accepted remedy for "ague," or malaria, once common in the hot, damp, mosquito-infested parts of our own country.

For the young Laura a trip to the store was an unforgettable thrill; sixty years after it happened she was able to recall every detail of her first one, including the storekeeper's gift of candy. Stores for her would always mean candy—not the brown or golden stuff of patty pans and sugaring-off time, but exotic flavors like horehound; exotic shapes like canes and ribbons; and all colors of the rainbow in stripes and flowers.

For Ma and Pa there might be the thrill of ogling novel merchandise like Cuban cigars, ready-hemmed napkins, and Ivory floating soap. For them it was also a time to be sharp. Package labels, where they existed, were long on boasts and short on information. The scale on which most purchases were measured bore no government inspection seal. They might not fear being "Yankeed" by storekeepers, though farmers were naturally suspicious of a man who bought produce at one price and sold it higher without moving his muscles. But the Pure Food and Drugs Act of 1906 was a long way off, and both merchant and customer were vulnerable. There was no law against stretching flour with plaster, cornmeal with sawdust, and pepper with gypsum. The coffee might easily contain dyed navy beans, the raisins might be part pebbles, and the lard might be floured. Trust your eyes, ears, nose, fingers, and maybe old friends —that was a good rule for frontier life, and especially for shopping at the country store.

About Cornmeal and Drippings, Then and Now

The recipes that follow call for stoneground cornmeal, because it is closest to what Ma used. Also called buhrground and waterground, it is whole corn crushed fine between stone grinding wheels that were usually powered by a waterwheel. It comes in varying textures and must be kept cool because of its oil content.

"New process" cornmeal, like our all-purpose flour, has had the germ removed to facilitate milling in high-speed steel rollers, and is enriched to restore food values lost in the processing. As a housewife Laura Wilder probably welcomed this modern cornmeal for its keeping qualities and a fine texture that made for better "raising."

Both old and new process cornmeal can be found in yellow and white. Yellow cornmeal is traditionally associated with New England, and white with southern cooking, although true Rhode Island "jonny-cakes" were always white. The Ingallses surely knew both colors and found, as we find, little difference in the flavors.

The "drippings" frequently called for are fat saved from

frying bacon and salt pork. Drippings were used for frying and often took the place of butter as a spread for bread. If they were to be used for pastry, the strong salty, smoky flavor was first removed by "clarifying," or boiling the fat briefly with an equal quantity of water. Chilling would then produce a block of clean, bland fat suspended over a flavored waste liquid.

Today drippings have been largely replaced by butter, cooking oils, and solid shortenings extracted from various seeds (corn, cotton, soy) by a process invented in our century.

FRIED SALT PORK WITH GRAVY; DRIPPINGS

Outdoors was crisp and cold. Sunshine gilded the frosty windows, and in the house everyone was hearty and cheerful. How the travelers did enjoy that breakfast! They praised everything they ate . . . the slices of fat pork were thin and crisp, and the gravy was smooth and brown and creamy. There was hot brown-sugar syrup, and plenty of fragrant steaming tea.

"This meat is delicious," Reverend Stuart said. "I know it is just fat salt pork, but I never tasted any like it. Would you tell me how you cook it, Sister Ingalls?"

BY THE SHORES OF SILVER LAKE

Salt pork is a fitting opener to this recipe collection. In the days before refrigerated rail cars opened the way for year-round distribution of fresh meat, preserved pork was the most common meat and fat source in the farm kitchen. Barrels of salt pork were a fixture of the country store, and the Ingallses came to depend on them after they no longer had pigs of their own.

Salt pork and bacon come from the fat belly that covers the spareribs of a hog. Both are preserved in a mixture of salt, sugar, and saltpeter. For salt pork the mixture is liquid, a brine. Bacon is usually dry-cured and smoked. The drippings from fried salt pork and bacon did for many a pioneer family what we now do with butter, margarine, solid vegetable fat, and vegetable oil.

Here are the directions Ma gave to Reverend Stuart. "I never measure," she said, "but I guess I can make a stab at it.

"The meat is easy. Cut the slices thin, and set them to parboil in cold water. When the water boils, pour it off. Then roll the slices in flour and fry them brown. When they are crisp, take them out onto a platter, and pour some of the fat off. Save it to use for butter. Then brown some flour in the fat left in the frying pan, pour in some milk, and keep stirring it as it boils until the gravy is just right."

This is what we have done in trying to re-create the recipe she wrote out.

For six servings you will need:
Salt pork, $\frac{1}{2}$ to 1 pound
White flour, $\frac{1}{2}$ cup unbleached all-purpose
Homogenized milk, 1 to $1\frac{1}{2}$ cups
Salt and pepper

Skillet, 12-inch; container for drippings

Parboil slices in the skillet, then drain skillet well before using it for frying. To produce crisp slices fry them well, at least 8 minutes to a side. Remove them to a platter and pour all but a tablespoon of fat into the container. Store fat drippings in a cool place for use in other recipes.

For gravy thickening use 2 tablespoons of the flour used for dredging. Blend the flour and fat very well before adding milk. Remove skillet from heat as soon as gravy bubbles and thickens. Taste before seasoning with salt and pepper. Serve gravy in a bowl and salt pork slices on a platter.

HASTY PUDDING

But for supper Grandma made hasty pudding.

She stood by the stove, sifting the yellow corn meal from her fingers into a kettle of boiling, salted water. She stirred the water all the time with a big wooden spoon, and sifted in the meal until the kettle was full of a thick, yellow, bubbling mass. Then she set it on the back of the stove where it would cook slowly. . . .

Then Uncle George came with a smaller bucket of syrup, and everybody ate the hot hasty pudding with maple syrup for supper.

LITTLE HOUSE IN THE BIG WOODS

The name goes back to English hasty pudding, made with oatmeal or wheat flour, which may have been a substitute for a very slow-cooking dish. Early Americans adapted it to cornmeal. Although the ingredients are simple, the cooking is tricky. Despite the name, the meal must be added slowly to prevent lumping, and the mixture must be cooked slowly to prevent scorching.

If you think this sounds plain and dull, try it as the Ingallses ate it, with pure maple syrup.

For six small servings you will need:
Salt, 1 teaspoon
Cornmeal, 1 cup stoneground yellow
Syrup

Kettle, 3-quart; bowl, 1-pint

Bring 4 cups of water to a boil in the kettle, and stir in salt. Put the meal in the bowl so you can gather it up easily in your hand. Proceed as Grandma did, stirring the water with a spoon in one hand and sprinkling in the meal with the other hand. When all the meal has been stirred in, reduce heat and simmer for at least 1 hour, stirring every 10 minutes to prevent burning and to test thickness. The pudding is done when it looks like cooked oatmeal.

Serve in bowls with syrup or pour into a deep dish to chill for Fried Cornmeal Mush (following recipe).

FRIED CORNMEAL MUSH

Breakfast was ready. When Pa came back from the creek they all sat by the fire and ate fried mush and prairie-chicken hash. Pa said he would make a door that very day. He wanted more than a quilt between them and the wolves, next time.

LITTLE HOUSE ON THE PRAIRIE

Cornmeal mush is hasty pudding. Fried mush is hasty pudding that has been chilled, sliced, and fried in fat. The Ingallses ate it often for breakfast, sometimes with maple syrup, sometimes with prairie-hen gravy, sometimes with molasses.

For six servings you will need:
Hasty Pudding (preceding recipe)
Drippings, 2 tablespoons

Mold—deep dish, loaf pan, or can; skillet, 12-inch

The night before serving prepare the mush, cooking it as thick and dry as possible. Pour it into a wet mold and chill overnight. A good improvised mold is an empty 1½-pound can: in the morning you can remove the bottom and push the contents out $\frac{1}{2}$ inch at a time for easy slicing into rounds.

If you use a dish or pan, turn the firm mush out and cut in ½-inch slices. Heat drippings in skillet and fry slices until golden brown on both sides.

JOHNNY-CAKE

Laura always wondered why bread made of corn meal was called johnny-cake. It wasn't cake. Ma didn't know, unless the Northern soldiers called it johnny-cake because the people in the South, where they fought, ate so much of it. They called the Southern soldiers Johnny Rebs. Maybe, they called the Southern bread, cake, just for fun.

Ma had heard some say it should be called journey-cake. She didn't know. It wouldn't be very good bread to take on a journey.

LITTLE HOUSE IN THE BIG WOODS

If Laura had ever heard a New Englander pronounce the word "journey" she would not have been puzzled. This rude bread goes back to colonial travelers who made a paste of cornmeal and water, spread it on a board, and baked it before an open fire. Rhode Islanders, who spell it "jonny-cake," cook the mixture as a griddle cake.

By the time of Laura's girlhood in Wisconsin in the early 1870s there were many recipes, plain and fancy, for the same product—a crusty slab of cooked cornmeal that was mostly a vehicle for syrup or gravy. At a threshers' dinner it may have helped make up for a shortage of forks.

For six servings you will need:
Cornmeal, 2 cups stoneground white or yellow
Salt, 1 teaspoon
Baking soda, 1 teaspoon
Drippings, 2 tablespoons
Molasses, 2 tablespoons
Cultured buttermilk, 1 cup

Bowl, 2-quart; baking sheet

In the bowl mix well the cornmeal, salt, and baking soda. Place drippings in the center. Stir molasses into $\frac{1}{2}$ cup boiling water, and pour the mixture on the drippings. Stir until drippings are melted and meal mixture becomes a paste. Stir in the buttermilk and mix well. Grease the baking sheet and pour the batter onto it, spreading it evenly by tilting the sheet or by pressing with a wet hand.

Preheat oven to 400°F. Bake for 20 to 30 minutes, until dough surface is cracked and edges are browned. Remove from the pan before it cools.

Some oldtime cooks insist that johnny-cakes be broken into serving portions, but cutting into squares seems a better way to assure fair shares.

Serve warm with honey, molasses, baked beans, or boiled cabbage and meat.

CORN DODGERS

That morning Mary and Laura played by the creek, among the rushes. They did not go near the swimming-hole. They did not touch the straw-stack. At noon they ate the corn dodgers and molasses and drank the milk that Ma had left for them. They washed their tin cups and put them away.

ON THE BANKS OF PLUM CREEK

Corn dodgers are a descendant of the Indians' *appone,* or corn pone—small cakes baked directly in the fireplace embers, with or without a wrapping of wet corn husks. In the Midwest, dodgers were usually made of cornmeal, lard, and milk. They were shaped either in small patties or like miniature ears of corn and were baked, fried, or fried *and* baked.

Dodgers take some getting used to, but they are worth trying —both hot, with butter, as they appeared at Thanksgiving, and cold, with molasses, as the girls ate them. Which do you prefer?

For 1 dozen dodgers you will need:
Cornmeal, 2 cups yellow stoneground
Salt, 1 scant teaspoon
Lard, 1 tablespoon
Homogenized milk, $\frac{1}{2}$ cup whole
Drippings, bacon or salt pork, 1 tablespoon

Bowl, 2-quart; skillet, 12-inch

Mix cornmeal and salt in bowl. Press lard into well in center. Bring $\frac{1}{2}$ cup of water to a boil, pour it on the lard, and stir after lard has melted. Stir until mixture is cool and crumbly, and then stir in enough milk to form a sticky batter, about $\frac{1}{2}$ cup.

Heat about 1 tablespoon of drippings in skillet. Shape the paste with hands into "corn ears," or drop it by the spoonful into hot skillet and press with spoon into cakes, watching out for hot spattering fat. Fry ears or cakes well on one side; turn and brown well on the other. Cook about 15 minutes in all.

CORNBREAD

> *Ma rolled up her sleeves and washed her hands and mixed corn-*
> *bread, while Mary brought the wood and Laura set the table. She set*
> *a tin plate and knife and fork and cup for Pa, and the same for Ma,*
> *with Carrie's little tin cup beside Ma's. And she set tin plates and*
> *knives and forks for her and Mary, but only their one cup between the*
> *plates.*
>
> *Ma made the cornmeal and water into two thin loaves, each shaped*
> *in a half circle. She laid the loaves with their straight sides together*
> *in the bake-oven, and she pressed her hand flat on top of each loaf. Pa*
> *always said he did not ask any other sweetening, when Ma put the*
> *prints of her hands on the loaves.*
>
> **LITTLE HOUSE ON THE PRAIRIE**

Cornbread, corn cakes, and game carried the Ingallses through their year on the Kansas prairie, where they had no garden to provide vegetables. The bread and cakes differed only in shape; the ingredients were always the same—cornmeal, salt, and water. And yet the flavors varied. Sometimes bacon fat was used in the pan, sometimes salt pork fat. The corn cakes were served sometimes hot and sometimes cold. At times they were eaten with molasses; at other times with prairie-hen gravy. Laura never spoke of this diet as monotonous; only hunger was tiresome.

For six servings you will need:
Drippings or pork rind
Cornmeal, 3 cups stoneground yellow
Salt, 1 teaspoon

Bake-oven, 4-quart, or skillet with ovenproof handles, 10-inch;
    bowl, 2-quart

Grease the skillet or bake-oven well with drippings or pork rind. Heat the oven to 400°F.

Mix cornmeal and salt in bowl. Pour in 1 cup of boiling water and stir. Add more boiling water, $\frac{1}{4}$ cup at a time, until you have a stiff dough that can be shaped with the hands.

Divide the dough, shape it, and press it into the greased bake-oven as Ma did. Cover and bake until dough surface is crusty, 30 to 40 minutes. Cut loaves in wedges and serve warm with more drippings or molasses.

CRACKLING CORNBREAD

Royal and Almanzo, working to fill the icehouse in Malone, listed "crackling cornbread" among their favorite foods. They were not speaking of the plain cornbread Laura knew in Kansas. With plenty of milk and butter at hand, Mother Wilder would have turned out a richer product. We doubt she would have used baking powder, a relatively new product, or sugar, with maple syrup, molasses, honey, and so many delicious preserves to add at the table.

For sixteen 2-inch squares you will need:
Butter, $\frac{1}{4}$ cup
Cornmeal, 2 cups stoneground yellow
Salt, 1 teaspoon
Baking soda, 1 teaspoon
Cracklings (see page 146), 2–3 tablespoons
Cultured buttermilk, 2 cups
Eggs, 2

Baking pan, 8-inch square; bowl, 2-quart; bowl, 1-pint

Preheat oven to 425°F. Melt butter by heating it briefly in baking pan.

In the larger bowl mix cornmeal, salt, baking soda, and cracklings. Stir in buttermilk. Beat eggs well in small bowl and add them to batter. Stir in the melted butter last. Pour batter into hot greased pan and bake about 30 minutes, until brown edges pull away from pan and the center of the bread bounces back when pressed. Cut in 2-inch squares and remove from pan before bread cools. Serve warm.

BAKED BEANS

The hot soup and hot tea warmed them all. They ate the broth from the beans. Then Ma emptied the beans into a milk-pan, set the bit of fat pork in the middle, and laced the top with dribbles of molasses. She set the pan in the oven and shut the oven door. They would have baked beans for supper.

THE LONG WINTER

The baked beans that often appeared in "Little House" meals suggest Ma's New England heritage. The dish goes back to beans cooked by Indians with bear grease and maple syrup in earth pits heated by hot stones.

Puritan housewives mixed beans with a bit of molasses, salt pork, and onion and sent them off in large pots to the local bakery to cook all Saturday. The beans would provide a hot Saturday supper and cold meals for a work-free Sabbath.

Beans are a good source of protein, economical of the earth's resources as well as our own. Preparing them the old way, with little molasses to mask the bean flavor, is worth a try. You may enrich the mixture, as Mother Wilder did, with onions and sliced peppers, but do sample the old-fashioned flavor before adding any more sweetening.

For six servings and leftovers you will need:
Navy, pea, or "little white" beans, 3 cups
Baking soda, 1 teaspoon
Salt pork, $\frac{1}{4}$ to $\frac{1}{2}$ pound
Molasses, $\frac{1}{4}$ cup
Optional:
Onions, 3 small, cut in chunks
Green peppers, 2, cut in strips
Additional molasses

Saucepan or kettle, 3-quart; milk pan, 10-inch

The night before cooking, put beans in saucepan or kettle to soak in water to cover (1 quart or more).

Next morning change the water and simmer for 5 minutes. Stir in baking soda and watch it fizz. Continue to simmer. After about 40 minutes test for tenderness: when the skins of two beans held in a spoon crack as you blow on them, they are done.

Pour the cloudy yellowish liquid off the tender beans, cover with 5 cups fresh water and return to simmer, adding salt pork that has been slashed to expose more surface. In 30 minutes this liquid will be ready to pour off, either to use in Bean Soup (following recipe) or to add later to the beans.

Grease milk pan with the cooked salt pork. Leave pork in pan and pour in beans. If you are adding vegetables, distribute them around pan. Dribble on $\frac{1}{4}$ cup of molasses, add water or bean broth just to cover, and put in oven.

The baking temperature will depend on when you want to serve the beans. At 250°F they will take about 8 hours to brown nicely; at 350°F only 4 hours are needed. In either case you may need to add more water as the beans cook, since they should not dry out until the last hour of baking.

Serve with a small pitcher of molasses to accommodate modern palates. Leftover beans may be used in Bean Porridge (page 28).

BEAN SOUP

There was nothing to do but sit huddled in coats and shawls, close to the stove.

"I'm glad I put beans to soak last night," said Ma. She lifted the lid of the bubbling kettle and quickly popped in a spoonful of soda. The boiling beans roared, foaming up, but did not quite run over.

"There's a little bit of salt pork to put in them too," Ma said.

Now and then she spooned up a few beans and blew on them. When their skins split and curled, she drained the soda-water from the kettle and filled it again with hot water. She put in the bit of fat pork.

"There's nothing like good hot bean soup on a cold day," said Pa.

THE LONG WINTER

This is not, alas, a recipe for the soup that is a thick, savory blend of corned beef liquor, puréed pea beans, chopped onions, celery fried in drippings, and tomatoes. The Ingallses may have dreamed of such soup during the Long Winter, but the best they had was the broth of beans simmered for baking.

If you wish to sample bean soup as the Ingallses knew it, start by preparing the preceding recipe for Baked Beans, and tasting the broth. How good a soup it is will depend largely on how cold you are, and how hungry.

BEAN PORRIDGE

And they played Bean Porridge Hot. Facing each other, they clapped their hands together and against each other's hands, keeping time while they said,

> *"Bean porridge hot,*
> *Bean porridge cold,*
> *Bean porridge in the pot,*
> *Nine days old. . . .*

> *"I like it hot,*
> *I like it cold,*
> *I like it in the pot,*
> *Nine days old."*

That was true. No supper was so good as the thick bean porridge, flavored with a small bit of salt pork, that Ma dipped onto the tin plates when Pa had come home cold and tired from his hunting. Laura liked it hot, and she liked it cold, and it was always good as long as it lasted. But it never really lasted nine days. They ate it up before that.

LITTLE HOUSE ON THE PRAIRIE

In early times pea beans were sometimes called "pease," which is why some of us know this chant as "Pease Porridge Hot." The dish referred to is a colonial one made by cooking pea beans, cornmeal, and hulled corn in the stock of boiled corned beef. The beans might be leftover baked beans. On the prairie Ma did without hulled corn and used salt pork for meat.

It is said that New England lumbermen, working on the coldest days of winter when the trees were easiest to fell, carried with them rounds of frozen bean porridge which they cut up and heated for dinner. They may well have found that it was best "nine days old."

For six servings you will need:
Salt pork, $\frac{1}{4}$ pound
Baked Beans (page 26), 1 to 2 cups
Cornmeal, 4 tablespoons stoneground yellow
Salt and pepper

Kettle, 3-quart; chopper and bowl; bowl, 1-pint

Heat 2 quarts of water to simmer in the kettle. Slice the salt pork; then chop it up in bowl. Transfer the pork pieces to the kettle and simmer 15 minutes. Stir the leftover baked beans into the kettle and simmer uncovered for another 30 minutes, stirring occasionally. A half hour before serving, dampen the cornmeal thoroughly with a few tablespoons of water, then stir it slowly into the porridge. Simmer for another 30 minutes to thicken. Add salt and pepper to taste. Ladle into soup plates and serve.

OYSTER SOUP

First, there was oyster soup. In all her life Laura had never tasted anything so good as that savory, fragrant, sea-tasting hot milk, with golden dots of melted cream and black specks of pepper on its top, and the little dark canned oysters at its bottom. She sipped slowly, slowly from her spoon, to keep that taste going over her tongue as long as she could.

And with this soup, there were little round oyster crackers. The little oyster crackers were like doll-crackers, and they tasted better because they were so light and small.

BY THE SHORES OF SILVER LAKE

Oysters have been a favorite American delicacy since before the arrival of the first Europeans. As East Coast cities grew, so did the number of oyster houses and street stalls where people snacked on freshly opened raw oysters. Wealthy midwesterners had barrels of oysters in ice sent by wagon from the Chesapeake Bay over the Allegheny Mountains.

The first canneries were built near oyster ports, and it was their output that the inland pioneers knew. In those days shellfish were scraped up from the sea bottoms of eastern and Gulf coastal waters where Nature had put them. But oyster farming became necessary to meet the demand, and many present-day varieties have been brought to our shores from Japan and Europe.

To Laura Ingalls such rich fare as this was a thrilling change from pork fat and cornmeal. Modern readers trying to avoid rich food may prefer to make oyster soup as Ma did on Christmas day during the Long Winter. For that cold celebration she had oysters, but no more than a cup of milk, no butter, and no oyster crackers.

For six small servings of rich soup you will need:
Oysters, two 8-ounce cans
Oyster crackers
Butter, 1 tablespoon
Homogenized milk, 2 cups
Light or heavy cream, 1 cup
Ground mace, a pinch
Ground nutmeg, a pinch
Ground pepper, a pinch

Measuring cup; saucepan or kettle, 3-quart

Drain liquid from oysters into measuring cup and add water to make 1 cup liquid. Heat this liquid in saucepan or kettle with another cup of water. Crush enough oyster crackers to produce $\frac{1}{2}$ cup of fine crumbs, and stir them, along with butter, into hot liquid. When boiling starts, add oysters and simmer 1 to 2 minutes. Add milk, cream, mace, nutmeg, and pepper, and return just to boil. Remove from heat and ladle into bowls. Serve with side dish of oyster crackers.

CODFISH BALLS

[Mrs. Woodworth] brought then a platter full of hot, creamy, brown codfish balls, and then a plate of tiny, hot biscuits. She passed butter in a round glass butter dish.

Mrs. Woodworth urged generous helpings, not once, but twice. Then she brought cups of coffee, and passed the cream and sugar.

LITTLE TOWN ON THE PRAIRIE

In the days before 1924, when Clarence Birdseye devised a way to flash-freeze fish, ocean fish headed for inland markets had to be salted, smoked, or canned (sometimes all three). Cod taken from the Atlantic by New England fishermen was put in brine, then drained and packed in long flat wooden boxes for shipment all over the country. Salt cod was a staple food.

Now there is no longer an American cod packing industry, and salt cod from Canada is an expensive luxury. It can still be found in boxes, one-pound size, as well as plastic vacuum bags. The brittle sun-dried bacalao of Italy and Spanish countries, now widely available in U.S. cities, requires longer soaking than this recipe allows.

We suggest you prepare codfish balls for breakfast, as New Englanders enjoy them. You will have to rise early, but your family will sleep through the odor of simmering cod that belies the delicacy of the finished dish.

For six servings (about five codfish balls each) you will need:
Moist salt cod, $\frac{1}{2}$ pound
Vinegar, 1 teaspoon
Potatoes, 1 pound
Eggs, 2 medium
Pepper
Lard, 1 pound

Bowl, 2-quart; saucepan, 6-cup; saucepan, 1-quart; slotted
    spoon; brown paper

The night before serving, cover cod in bowl with tap water, add vinegar, and let soak at room temperature.

Next morning wash and peel the potatoes and place in larger saucepan. Simmer in water to cover until they break easily with a fork, about 20 to 25 minutes. While potatoes cook, drain the cod and flake it into the smaller saucepan: start by removing any tough skin; then pull flesh apart in small pieces. Cover cod with water and simmer 15 minutes. Drain well and cool.

Rinse out the bowl, break the eggs into it, and beat them well with a fork. Break up the potatoes as you turn up the heat to cook away any remaining water. Remove from burner and mash with slotted spoon until smooth and cool. Turn potatoes and cod into bowl and beat well with eggs and pepper.

Rinse potato saucepan and wipe until completely dry. Heat lard in it until it is hot enough to brown a ½-inch cube of sliced bread in a minute (325°F). Drop the codfish mixture in the hot fat by rounded teaspoonfuls, four or five at a time. The balls should brown in 1 to 1½ minutes. Remove them when brown to a warm plate with brown paper to drain. Repeat with remaining mixture. Before serving remove the paper from the plate.

Chapter 4

Foods from the Woods,
Wilds, and Waters

OF ALL THE FOODS eaten by the Ingallses, it is the wild ones that bring us closest to the flavors they knew. In the century since their time, science and industry have changed the growing and milling of wheat, the cultivation of garden vegetables, the breeding of cattle and swine, and the nature of confections. But wild blueberries are still wild blueberries; jack rabbits are still jack rabbits. The supply has changed, however, along with our relationship to it.

In spite of the Ingallses' best efforts at farming, it was Nature and her gifts that sustained them through much of Laura's childhood. In the Big Woods deer furnished them with meat, and maple trees yielded sweetening. The pelts of muskrat, mink, and otter, caught in Pa's traps, were traded for tools and cloth and coffee.

Many who went west thought the supply endless. Pa knew better. When he found a beaver meadow he "did not set traps because there were so few beavers left"—the result, we can assume, of their having both a valuable pelt and a delicious tail. The wild turkey that the first white colonists found in such abundance had disappeared from Wisconsin by the time Laura was five. Farther west, we are told, buffalo were once so plentiful they were slaughtered for their tongues alone. Gradually, with the expansion of rail lines, the fine flavor of buffalo steak became known and sought after. Pursuit became big business until, by the end of the century, there were no more buffalo herds to pursue.

To their good fortune, the Ingallses found the Kansas prairie alive with rabbits, prairie hens, and berries; the Minnesota streams full of fish; and the Dakota marshlands abundant with ducks and geese. But they would never again find the variety and abundance of wildlife that the Wisconsin woods sheltered, or the maple sugar from the trees themselves.

This is not to suggest a steady decline in game resources over the years. Between the Ingallses' time and ours the balance of nature has undergone many shifts. The clearing of the land for farming, railroads, and highways destroyed the natural habitat of many animals. Predators and farmers protecting their crops destroyed the animals themselves. Some, like the pesky passenger pigeon, were pursued to extinction.

At the same time conservation efforts gained momentum. By the end of the nineteenth century the first state and national forest preserves were established. These and our national parks became sanctuaries for all forms of wildlife. Both state and federal governments adopted laws limiting hunting to a sport and restricting killing to "seasons." They have used hunting license fees to finance breeding and "stocking" programs that ensure a constant population of sport fish and fowl.

A star conservation example is the wild turkey, brought back from near-extinction by Pennsylvania game officials who learned how to breed the wily bird in captivity and released him into state forests where he could roost and forage undisturbed. Because there are now enough wild turkeys to permit hunting under careful regulation we include a recipe. There is none for the prairie chicken, even though five states have enough of these grouse to permit some hunting.

Sometimes the advance of civilization favors wildlife. Utility and highway rights-of-way have encouraged the spread of wild grapevines and berry bushes and the mammals that browse on them. In suburbia, white-tail deer feed on ornamental shrubbery, and raccoons feast in household garbage cans. We are learning again what the Indians knew when they set fire to shaded forests—that clearing one kind of growth can make way for another.

And what about the flavor of wild things—has that changed

along with the supply? We can only guess. Wildlife management has certainly made some alterations. Favorite sport fish like trout are now commonly bred in state-operated hatcheries and released into local streams, sometimes as fingerlings and sometimes as adults fed on a diet of liver and vitamins. Most states have commercial game preserves where sportsmen can pay to pursue guaranteed quarry. Usually the pheasants, quail, and ducks are grain-fed, and there is a freezer full of ready-to-eat dressed specimens for those who want to exchange their fresh kill.

In fact, modern flash-freezing and shipping have broadened our access to many fresh wild flavors. Fish and fowl frozen directly after killing have no chance to develop the "fishy" and "gamy" taints often complained of in the past.

Blueberries and cranberries can still be found in the wild in cool climates. Most processed blueberries—those sold in ice cream, preserves, and baked goods—come from vast barrens in Maine where the wild lowbush berry is tended and fertilized. The large blueberries sold fresh by the dry pint are hybrids of recent development. Store cranberries come from New England stock that has been transplanted to New Jersey, Wisconsin, and Oregon, among other states. These berries, too, are bigger and juicier than truly wild ones because the plants are fertilized and tended.

Pa often found it was less work to gather food than to grow it. The reverse is true today, and wild flavors that must be pursued are costly. In New York and Vermont, which furnish half the country's maple syrup, plastic pipelines to a central collector have replaced many tree buckets, but it still takes forty gallons of sap to produce one of maple syrup. Rising labor and fuel costs have made a luxury of the Ingallses' everyday sweetener. In these recipes, we yield, reluctantly, to the poor man's substitute, maple flavoring.

Preparing and Preserving Wild Foods

Before any meat could be prepared for a meal or preserved for the future, the animal first had to be "dressed." How we take that term for granted! Not so the hunter, who first of all, in the case of ducks or grouse, must "draw" the birds as soon as possible after

shooting, removing the crop and entrails. The crop, throat, and
stomach would go to animals; the entrails (liver, heart, and gizzard)
would become "giblets" for gravy. Next a drawn bird was hung by
its feet to bleed for an hour or two. Then the housewife took over:
she plucked the feathers by her favorite method, either dry or after
scalding the bird in hot water. Pinfeathers and hair were burned off,
or singed. Finally, after a bath in vinegar water to remove all blood
traces, the bird was ready to be stuffed for roasting or cut up for
stewing.

To preserve meat and fruit for later use, the Ingallses had
three choices besides freezing—smoking, salting, and drying.
Our instructions here are limited to those for drying, a simple
technique done with simple equipment and in little time. Those
who happen to have freshly killed deer and want to produce
smoked venison should read the first chapter of *Little House in the
Big Woods.* It tells just how Pa skinned a deer, cut up the meat,
and salted both hide and flesh. Using a section of a hollow tree,
he built a smokehouse, where he hung the salted meat on nails
high inside. On the floor he built a smoldering fire of hickory
chips and moss. Smoke filled the house and escaped the cracks;
when it thinned, Laura and Ma fed the fire with more chips. Finally the venison was ready to be wrapped in paper and hung in
the attic, and the fire was allowed to die. The whole process
took three to four weeks.

Fish were often dry-cured and smoked like venison, but Pa
Ingalls's catch from Lake Pepin, we're told, was "salted down in
barrels for the winter." For a wagonload of fish, "some as big as
Laura," this was quite a job. First the fish were scaled, the organs
removed, and the flesh cut from the skeletons. Then the meat was
layered in barrels with quantities of salt, saltpeter, and spices. In
time the salted moist meat produced a brine that had to be fresh-
ened by boiling. The fish then had to be unpacked, rinsed in fresh
water, and returned to the barrel with the boiled brine. Today most
fish preserved by sportsmen and commercial fishermen are fast
frozen, and pickled fish are no longer a poor second to fresh ones
but an expensive delicacy. They are another example of yesterday's
commonplace becoming today's special treat.

STEWED JACK RABBIT AND DUMPLINGS

It was a big day on the Kansas prairie. With Mr. Edwards's help, Pa managed to finish the house, all but the roof. Because they had company, Ma cooked "an especially good supper . . . of stewed jack rabbit with white-flour dumplings and plenty of gravy."

Don't let your fear for the fate of the jack rabbit keep you from enjoying this fine meal if you have the chance. This long-legged, long-eared fellow and his cousin the cottontail are among

America's most durable citizens. After centuries of pursuit by animals and humans, they flourish to the extent that many states permit year-round hunting. As plant-eaters they are a pest to farmers.

If you can't find a hunter to give you a skinned rabbit (he will want the pelt), look for a farm-raised rabbit at a German butcher shop (*Hasenpfeffer* is a favorite German dish) or for packaged frozen pieces at the supermarket. Your stew will be all white meat.

For six servings you will need:
A rabbit, 3 pounds, dressed, with giblets
Salt pork, 6 ounces
Flour, 2 tablespoons, unbleached all-purpose
White-Flour Dumplings (page 73)

Saucepan, 1-quart; chopper and bowl; bake-oven or covered
    casserole, 4-quart; skillet, 6-inch; bowl, 2-quart, for dough

Thaw frozen rabbit according to package directions or ask hunter or butcher to cut the rabbit into eight serving pieces (two forelegs, two rib sections, two backs, and two hind legs).

Simmer giblets in saucepan with 2 cups of water.

Slice salt pork and dice it with the chopper. Brown the diced pieces in the bake-oven or casserole over medium heat; remove the pieces and save.

Brown the rabbit pieces in the pork fat in the bake-oven, taking care to avoid spattering fat. This will take 10 to 15 minutes. Add the saucepan liquid; cover the bake-oven and simmer for 35 to 40 minutes.

Meanwhile prepare gravy thickening. In the skillet, over medium heat, toast the flour until it resembles cocoa powder, stirring constantly to prevent burning. This will take 10 to 15 minutes. Let flour cool in skillet.

Remove giblets from saucepan to the chopping bowl and chop fine. Return them to saucepan, add browned flour, and work to a paste. Slowly blend in 1 cup of water.

As the stew continues to simmer, prepare dumpling dough according to recipe.

When the meat is just tender, stir diced salt pork and saucepan gravy into the bake-oven. With a soupspoon, drop the dough onto the bubbling liquid, covering the surface. Let simmer on medium-low heat until dumplings puff and lose their gloss (about 10 minutes). Cover with a lid, reduce heat to low, and simmer another 10 minutes, until dumplings are cooked through.

Serve as Ma did, with cornbread and molasses.

SPIT-ROASTED WILD DUCK

He had brought four fat ducks, and he said he could have killed hundreds. But four were all they needed. He said to Ma, "You save the feathers from the ducks and geese we eat, and I'll shoot you a feather bed." . . .

Pa went whistling to mix mud and cut green sticks and build the chimney up again, while Ma cleaned the ducks. Then the fire merrily crackled, a fat duck roasted, and the cornbread baked. Everything was snug and cozy again.

LITTLE HOUSE ON THE PRAIRIE

The ducks Pa bagged were no doubt mallards. Having only one tin kitchen, Ma must have roasted them one or two at a time, saving some for future meals.

Our directions are for spit roasting wild ducks before an open fire with bricks, a skewer, and two pans taking the place of a tin kitchen. Beware of substitutions: a domestic duck is too fatty for this recipe and a spit mounted directly over charcoal won't do, for the juices will be lost to the fire.

However plump they may seem, wild ducks have little fat to moisten their dark flesh. Without salt pork to insert in it (called larding) or wine to marinate it, you may find the meat quite dry, but at least you will taste the natural flavor.

For six servings you will need:
Mallard ducks, 3, about 2 pounds each, dressed and thawed
White flour, about $\frac{1}{2}$ cup
Browned flour, 2 tablespoons (page 38)
Salt and pepper

Fire in fireplace; bricks, 6; dripping pans, 2; barbecue skewer,
   15-inch; saucepan, 1-pint; baking sheet; spider or skillet,
   10-inch; chopper and bowl

To start, your fire must be several hours old, with a good bed
of coals on the hearth.

Just in front of the coals stack the bricks in two columns a foot
apart to support the ends of the skewer-spit. Between the columns
and under the spit place a dripping pan. Stand the other pan on
edge in front of the brick columns to act as a reflector.

Rinse the ducks in cold water and shake dry. Run the skewer-
spit lengthwise through a duck so it is secure and will turn with the
spit.

Prop spitted duck on bricks before hot coals. In the pan below pour 1 cup of hot water. The pan will catch the drippings. Turn the bird every 10 minutes and baste with pan liquid.

Meanwhile rinse giblets (organs) and put them to simmer in the saucepan with 1 cup of water.

After half an hour of roasting remove duck on spit to baking sheet and dust with white flour. Return to the fire and continue to roast until legs move easily, another 15 minutes or so. After a final basting, remove bird to spider or skillet on hearth to keep warm. Proceed to roast remaining ducks. Replenish water in dripping pan as needed.

When broth has simmered an hour remove giblets. These may be chopped fine for the gravy, served whole with the ducks, or cut up for feeding to animals. To the cool broth add browned flour and basting liquid; stir over heat until the gravy bubbles and thickens slightly. Season with salt and pepper to taste, and pour in gravy bowl. Serve with ducks and cornbread.

BLACKBIRD PIE

She opened the oven door, and took out the tin milk pan. It was full of something covered thickly over with delicately browned biscuit crust. She set it before Pa and he looked at it amazed. "Chicken pie!"

" 'Sing a song of sixpence—' " said Ma. . . .

"Well, I'll be switched!" said Pa. He cut into the pie's crust with a big spoon, and turned over a big chunk of it onto a plate. The underside was steamed and fluffy. Over it he poured spoonfuls of thin brown gravy, and beside it he laid half a blackbird, browned, and so tender that the meat was slipping from the bones. He handed that first plate across the table to Ma. . . .

"The pan held twelve birds," said Ma. "Just two apiece, but one is all that Grace can possibly eat, so that leaves three for you, Charles."

"It takes you to think up a chicken pie, a year before there's chickens to make it with," Pa said. He ate a mouthful and said, "This beats a chicken pie all hollow."

LITTLE TOWN ON THE PRAIRIE

Blackbirds are still a nuisance to farmers, but only one member of this large group of birds may be freely hunted throughout the United States. This is the starling, a twentieth-century European immigrant that is despised by townspeople as well for its noisy, dirty massing habits. Starlings cannot be bought; they must be hunted.

The Ingallses' corn-fed blackbirds were apparently plump enough to fry in their own fat. Not so the starling, which is lean and tough like another pest, the bygone passenger pigeon. This recipe is therefore based on old directions for pigeon pie. Starlings have little meat to reward the effort of plucking, but what there is has rich game flavor even after long cooking.

For six servings you will need:
Starlings, 12, plucked and dressed
Yellow onion, 1 medium
Cloves, 2 whole
Browned flour, 2 tablespoons (page 38)
Salt and pepper
Sour-Milk Biscuits (page 73)

Meat cleaver or scissors; saucepan, 2-quart; bowl, 2-quart;
    pastry surface and rolling pin; milk pan, 10-inch

With meat cleaver or scissors cut birds in half along breastbone and backbone. Put birds, giblets, onion, and cloves in saucepan with 2 cups of water and simmer covered about 2 hours, or until a leg can easily be pulled from a test bird. About half the liquid will cook away.

Preheat oven to 400°F. Prepare biscuit dough, just moist enough to hold together in a ball.

Put the dough on the pastry surface and roll out, with as few strokes as possible, into a 10-inch circle $\frac{3}{8}$ inch thick.

Remove starlings and giblets from broth to milk pan. Discard onion and cloves. Stir browned flour into the broth and heat it to boiling for a minute or two, stirring the while. Salt and pepper the

slightly thickened broth and pour over the birds. Cover the pan with the biscuit crust.

Bake pie at 400°F for 10 minutes, then lower heat to 350° and bake 10 minutes more, or until crust is cooked through.

FRIED FISH

> *Laura and Pa went back to the house, carrying those flopping fish.
> Ma's eyes were round when she saw them. Pa cut off their heads and
> stripped out their insides and showed Laura how to scale fish. He scaled
> three, and she scaled almost all of one. Ma rolled them in meal and
> fried them in fat, and they all ate those good fish for supper. . . .*
>
> *Every morning after that, before he went to work, Pa brought fish
> from the trap. . . . He brought buffalo fish and pickerel, and catfish,
> and shiners, and bullheads with two black horns. He brought some
> whose names he did not know.*

ON THE BANKS OF PLUM CREEK

The small fish Pa and Laura trapped and the trout that Almanzo and his father caught were called pan fish because they were usually cooked in a frying pan. Ma Ingalls and Mother Wilder would have agreed with Lydia Child, who wrote in 1832 that such fish "relishes better to be fried after salt pork than to be fried in lard alone." They dredged their fish in cornmeal, partly to assure good gravy, but their fish were so fresh that they could afford to ignore Mrs. Child's other advice: "If you live remote from the seaport, and cannot get fish while hard and fresh, wet it with an egg beaten, before you meal it, to prevent its breaking."

If fishing season is past or you are far from fresh streams, a local store can probably supply you with pickerel or trout from commercial hatcheries. They will be close in flavor to game fish but larger and meatier.

For six servings you will need:
Salt pork, $\frac{1}{4}$ pound
Pan fish, 3–4 pounds, cleaned and scaled
Cornmeal, 1 to 2 cups
Salt and pepper
Homogenized milk, $1\frac{1}{2}$ cups
Vinegar

Skillet, 10-inch or 12-inch; dripping pan; spatula or turner

Slice salt pork and fry to a crisp brown over medium heat, about 5 minutes to a side. Remove the crisp slices to a warm serving platter.

Spread fish out in the dripping pan and sprinkle cornmeal over them. Turn and add meal until they are completely coated. Dust with salt and pepper.

Place in hot frying pan as many fish as will fit without touching. Fry over medium heat until brown on one side, about 5 minutes. Turn fish carefully, using spatula to unstick them, and fry another 5 to 8 minutes, until just tender. Remove them to warm platter.

Scrape loose any particles sticking to pan; fry remaining fish and transfer them to platter. Remove pan from heat and stir in milk vigorously. Return pan to heat just long enough for milk to foam up. Pour the gravy into a serving bowl. Serve with fish platter.

At the table sprinkle the fish with a few drops of vinegar before eating.

ROASTED WILD TURKEY
WITH CORNBREAD STUFFING

Turkeys were the centerpieces of at least two Ingalls Christmas dinners. The frozen one from Reverend Alden that arrived in DeSmet in May was surely a domestic one, but on the Kansas prairie Pa shot a wild turkey. "If it weighed less than twenty pounds, he said, he'd eat it, feathers and all."

Even when you find a flock, as Pa did, wild turkeys aren't easy to bag. They are elusive sprinters, best lured by waiting patiently in the woods and imitating their mating call. They are also a challenge to the cook. They are more flavorful than domestic turkeys, which have been greatly altered by breeding since they were taken from Mexico to Europe and brought back to North America. But wild turkeys have less fat and can become tough and dry.

This recipe is for wild turkey as Ma might have roasted it in a cookstove oven, using only the ingredients she had on hand after Pa's trip to Independence. In fact she had no oven, and a 20-pound bird would have collapsed the tin kitchen. What she probably did was to cut up the bird, steam the pieces in the bake-oven, and then roast them. With wild turkeys even rarer today than they were then, we can't recommend such treatment, particularly as it obscures the bird's distinctive shape. Our recipe is also for a smaller bird.

For eight servings, second helpings, and leftovers you will need:
A dressed wild turkey, about 12 pounds, fresh or frozen, with
    giblets
Salt pork, $\frac{3}{4}$ to 1 pound
Cornmeal, 6 cups stoneground white or yellow
Salt
Dried sage, $\frac{1}{4}$ cup crumbled
Pepper
Flour, $\frac{1}{2}$ cup all-purpose

Dripping pan, 6-quart; bowl, 6-quart; saucepan, 1-quart;
    chopper and bowl; skewers or darning needle and coarse
    thread; crock or tin for fat

If turkey is frozen, allow enough time for it to thaw completely. Meanwhile prepare cornbread for stuffing: grease the dripping pan with salt pork. Preheat the oven to 400°F.

To prepare stuffing mix cornmeal and 3 teaspoons salt in the bowl. Pour in 2 cups of boiling water and stir. Add more water, $\frac{1}{4}$ cup at a time, until you have a stiff dough that will stay together. Spread the dough out evenly in the pan, pressing with the hands. Bake until brown around the edges, about 20 to 30 minutes. Cool 10 minutes before removing from the pan.

Meanwhile simmer the giblets in the saucepan in 3 cups of water. After 10 minutes remove only the liver to drain and cool; continue simmering the rest for about an hour.

When the cornbread is thoroughly cool break it up fine in the bowl. Add a scant 2 cups of water and squeeze the bread to moisten it throughout. Cut salt pork into six or more thin slices and chop half of them fine. Chop the liver fine. Crush sage with fingers. Stir choppings and sage into bread with some salt and pepper.

Preheat the oven to 325°F. Rinse the bird and pat it dry. Pack stuffing loosely into neck opening and main cavity. Close neck by pulling skin over the opening and securing it with the wing tips behind the bird. Close the main opening with skewers or by sewing.

Grease the dripping pan and the bird with the slices of salt pork. Shake a coating of white flour over the skin, to seal it and enrich the gravy. Place the turkey breast up in the pan. Slip two slices of salt pork under the roast and place two slices on the breast. Place in the oven (Ma would have started the turkey with its breast down and turned it after an hour, but this difficult step can be omitted).

After 1 hour pour 1 cup of water over the turkey and dust it again with flour. After 2 hours raise the oven temperature to 350° and baste the roast well with pan liquid. Continue to baste every 20 minutes, adding water as needed.

Meanwhile remove the giblet broth from the stove to cool. Set aside the heart and gizzard as platter garnish. Use some of the liquid to make 2 tablespoons of flour into a paste, in a cup. Gradually blend the paste into the cool broth.

At 3 hours begin testing the turkey for doneness. "A sure

sign," says an old cookbook, "is the readiness of the joints to separate from the body." In other words, the legs should move freely.

Remove the roasted bird to a warm platter. Tilt the pan and skim any clear fat into the fat crock or tin. To finish the gravy, stir the broth into the dripping pan and loosen all the particles there. Heat just until the liquid boils up and thickens. Season with salt and pepper and put in a serving bowl. Serve the turkey and gravy with sweet potatoes baked in ashes and Salt-Rising Bread (page 75).

CRANBERRY JELLY

> *Laura did not need to be called next morning. She was up at dawn, and all day she helped Ma bake and stew and boil the good things for next day's Christmas dinner.*
>
> *Early that morning Ma added water and flour to the bread sponge and set it to rise again. Laura and Carrie picked over the cranberries and washed them. Ma stewed them with sugar until they were a mass of crimson jelly.*
>
> THE LONG WINTER

Massachusetts and Laura's home state of Wisconsin were for centuries the main source of wild cranberries enjoyed by the Indians and then by the colonists. By the time of Laura's youth, cultivation was under way in New Jersey and Wisconsin and just beginning in Oregon.

Both wild and cultivated cranberries can be tested for freshness by bouncing them (bad ones won't bounce). Good berries are now so widely available in the market that only the hardiest of foragers care to search the bogs on raw fall days for fruits hiding beneath low-growing vines, especially as they are much too sour to nibble along the way.

Cranberries were prized for their "jelling" qualities in the days before packaged gelatin.

For six servings you will need:
Cranberries, 1 pound
Granulated sugar, $2\frac{1}{2}$ cups

Kettle, 8-quart; mold or bowl, 1-quart

Pick over and wash the cranberries, discarding any soft ones. Place sugar and 1 cup of water in the kettle, and bring to a boil. Add berries and cook over medium heat about 15 minutes, stirring frequently. Pour into a wet mold or bowl and chill.

To unmold, place serving dish facedown on top of mold, invert so that dish is underneath mold, and shake gently. Remove mold and serve jelly with turkey.

BLUEBERRY PUDDING

Remember when Almanzo went berrying with his family and encountered a bear? So successful at berrying were they that "for every meal there was huckleberry pie or blueberry pudding," we are told.

In the long-ago days before supermarkets offered year-round fresh fruit and frozen sweets, and before home ovens opened the world of pies and layer cakes, puddings were the principal confection. Fruits and vegetables from coconuts to yams were mixed with a batter of sweetened flour or cornmeal, tied up in a cloth or hand-knit pudding bag, and boiled in a kettle over an open fireplace to produce puddings. Colonial housewives often cooked the pudding right over a bubbling stew.

In time, pudding bags gave way to tin molds and oven-baked puddings became the style. This old-fashioned recipe from an 1898 edition of the *Malone Cook Book* makes no concessions to the ovens or baking powder of the day.

For six servings you will need:
Blueberries, 1 dry pint or 10 ounces
Butter, 4 tablespoons, soft
Egg, 1
Homogenized milk, $\frac{3}{4}$ cup
Baking soda, $\frac{1}{2}$ teaspoon
White flour, $1\frac{1}{2}$ cups unbleached all-purpose
Granulated sugar, 1 cup
Cream of tartar, 1 teaspoon
Sauce for Blueberry Pudding (following recipe)

Pudding mold with lid, $1\frac{1}{2}$-quart, or coffee can, 2-pound; bowl,
    1-quart; bowl, 2-quart; deep kettle, 4-quart

Wash and drain blueberries, removing stems and bad fruit. Generously grease inside the mold or can and its lid with some of the soft butter (use greased foil to replace a plastic can lid).

In the smaller bowl beat the egg; stir in milk and baking soda. In the larger bowl mix flour, sugar, and cream of tartar; work in remaining butter with fingers until mixture is uniformly coarse. Stir liquid into dry mixture until all is moist. Stir in blueberries last with a few strokes, taking care not to crush the berries.

Pour blueberry batter into mold or can and cover tightly. Set the container in the kettle and fill kettle two-thirds full with boiling water. Cover and simmer for $1\frac{1}{2}$ hours or longer. As long as there is plenty of water in the kettle there is little danger that the pudding will overcook.

Unmold the finished pudding on a platter and serve with the sauce.

SAUCE FOR BLUEBERRY PUDDING

This light sauce is unusual in containing rose water, a flavoring—frequently homemade—that was once as well known in this country as it is today in the Middle East. By now it has been so thoroughly replaced by vanilla in American cooking that it is difficult to find, and you can use lemon juice instead.

For a pudding for six (previous recipe) you will need:
Granulated sugar, 1 cup
Butter, 3 tablespoons
Salt, a pinch
Ground nutmeg, a pinch
Rose water, 2 tablespoons

Saucepan, 1-quart

Simmer the sugar with 2 cups of water until it begins to thicken into syrup, about 10 minutes. Remove from heat and stir in remaining ingredients. Serve warm in a pitcher.

HUCKLEBERRY PIE

Early in the afternoon the bushel baskets and all the pails were full, and Father drove home. They were all a little sleepy, soaked in sunshine and breathing the fruity smell of the berries.

For days Mother and the girls made jellies and jams and preserves, and for every meal there was huckleberry pie or blueberry pudding.

FARMER BOY

At least three dozen species of blueberry can still be found growing wild across the United States, some peculiar to the East Coast and some native to the West. Americans often call some of these species "huckleberries," and that's apparently what the author did. The true huckleberry contains hard seeds—ten to a fruit—and would probably not be used for pies where blueberries were available.

Those who cannot go berrying will have to depend on cultivated blueberries, which are *never* called huckleberries and are fatter and less tangy than their wild forebears. They are also juicier and have thinner skins, so that thickening is needed to prevent them from bubbling over in the oven.

For a 9-inch pie (eight to ten servings) you will need:
Common Family Paste for Pies, double recipe (see page 194)
Blueberries or "huckleberries," 2 dry pints
Brown sugar, $\frac{3}{4}$ cup
White flour, 2 tablespoons unbleached all-purpose
Ground nutmeg, a pinch

Pie pan, 9-inch; colander; bowl, 2-quart

Line the pie pan with half the pie paste. Chill dough for a top crust.

Wash and pick over the berries, eliminating bad ones and stems. Drain in colander.

In the bowl mix brown sugar, flour, and nutmeg. Put half the berries into the bottom crust and strew half the sugar mixture on top. Add the remaining berries, mounding them toward the center, and top with the rest of the sugar mixture.

Preheat the oven to 425°F. Roll out the top crust, place it atop the fruit, and pinch the edges. Vent the crust with a slash or design and put the pie in the oven, reducing the heat to 400°. Bake about 40 minutes or until nicely browned.

NOTE: We endorse the advice of venerable cookbook author Eliza Leslie, which might have comforted the newlywed Laura in her first four years: "With fruit pies always have a sugar dish on the table, in case they should not be found sweet enough."

SUN-DRIED WILD FRUIT

When they came to a plum thicket they set down their big pails. They filled their little pails with plums and emptied them into the big pails till they were full. Then they carried the big pails back to the roof of the dugout. On the clean grass Ma spread clean cloths, and Laura and Mary laid the plums on the cloths, to dry in the sun. Next winter they would have dried plums to eat.

ON THE BANKS OF PLUM CREEK

Lack of sugar or containers for making preserves didn't keep Ma from laying by summer's bounty of wild fruits, either in Kansas (where she and the girls risked malaria to gather blackberries) or in Plum Creek. She turned to sun drying, an old home art now used largely by commercial growers.

Broad orange fields of apricots and peaches drying in the sun are a common sight in parts of California where there is little or no summer rainfall. It is the easiest preserving method available in dry climates.

To sun-dry summer fruits like plums, cherries, blackberries, and raspberries you can simply do as the Ingallses did, but the process will be surer and swifter if you take these extra precautions:

WASH the fruit if it has been exposed to chemical sprays or dusty winds. Drain it well.

SPLIT FRUITS WITH PITS, such as plums and cherries, and remove the pits.

USE PORTABLE, OFF-THE-GROUND SURFACES for spreading out your cloth and fruit. This improves air circulation and enables you to move fruit out of dew or rain. Stretch curtain cloth on frames set on carpenter horses or use coated or stainless screening (common galvanized house screens may impart lead).

COVER DRYING FRUIT with cheesecloth to keep off bees, other insects, and neighborhood pets.

REMOVE DRYING FRAMES BEFORE SUNSET to a porch, garage, or heater room for dry overnight storage. Return them outdoors after the morning dew has burned off, and check throughout the day to see that the moving sun has not cast them in shade.

Repeat this daily exposure for three days to a week, until the fruits have shriveled and can be squeezed without yielding juice. They will reduce to one-fourth to one-eighth their original weight. They will also darken, for natural color can be retained only by "sulfuring."

It is best to package fruits before they become brittle; fleshy fruits should be "leathery." Pack them in sterilized dry jars with screw lids or corks, leaving as little air space as possible. Store in a dark dry place and examine now and then. If there are any signs of mold, put dried fruit in a warm oven for an hour. This should kill the mold.

If you have no sunshine or lack yard space, don't despair. You can try indoor drying (see Dried Apples, page 128), or you can place your trays in a parked car with the windows open slightly (surely the pioneers used their covered wagons this way!).

STEWED DRIED FRUIT

The stewed dried blackberries shared with Mr. Edwards in Kansas, the stewed dried plums on the Thanksgiving table in Plum Creek, and the dried-raspberry sauce Mrs. Boast served with biscuits and honey on New Year's Day were all prepared in about the same way. Here are general rules for stewing dried wild fruits.

MEASURING

For dried berries allow about 1 to 2 ounces per person. For dried plums and apples allow about 3 to 4 ounces per person. Measure the volume of the fruit as you put it in the stew pan and add 1½ times the amount of water.

STEWING AND SOAKING

Overnight or all-day soaking produces the best stewed fruit. Oldtimers frequently soaked fruit before stewing, but it is far more effective to stew the fruit for 12 to 15 minutes, remove from heat, and let sit in covered pan. The fruit will continue to absorb cooking water.

SWEETENING

An hour before serving, taste the fruit. If it is not yet tender cook another 10 minutes. Add sugar to taste, a teaspoonful at a time —*before* you cook, if you are making a sauce and want to have thick syrup; *after* cooking, if you want the fruit to be as fresh-tasting as possible. Serve at room temperature.

If you have no dried fruit of your own but wish to prepare an authentic Plum Creek Thanksgiving dinner, try using prunes, which are moist-dried plums.

Jams, Jellies, and Preserves, Then and Now

The "dishes of jams and jellies and preserves" that graced Farmer Boy's table were the author's notion of bounty and luxury. They all employ the preserving power of sugar, cooked in generous amounts with fruit. It was the Ingallses' luck to have little sugar when wild fruit was plentiful, in Kansas and on Plum Creek, and to have only ground cherries and garden vegetables from Nature when sugar was at hand, in South Dakota.

Preserves are, properly speaking, fruits preserved whole in heavy syrup, but here and elsewhere the term is often used for jam, or fruit pulp cooked with sugar. Good jam is thick but not tacky and is close in color to the fresh fruit. Jelly is fruit juice cooked with sugar; it should be clear, brightly colored, firm but not rubbery, and slightly tart to the taste. Both depend for "jelling" on pectin, an ingredient naturally present in fruits in varying amounts. To preserve fruits low in pectin (apricots and peaches, for example) we can now buy pectin and add it. Our grandmothers, instead, often added some high-pectin fruit like crab apples.

These are the basic steps for sugar preserving. Some have changed greatly, some not at all:

SELECT UNRIPE AS WELL AS RIPE FRUIT. Mother Wilder and Ma knew that "green" fruit was best for preserving. We know it's because ripening reduces the pectin content. About half the fruit should be ripe for color and flavor.

FOR JAM: WEIGH OUT FRUIT AND SUGAR AND COOK TOGETHER QUICKLY. A turn-of-the-century cookbook says, "In the old way of preserving, we used pound for pound, when they were kept in stone jars or crocks; now, as most preserves are put up in sealed jars or cans, less sugar seems sufficient; three-quarters of a pound of sugar is generally all that is required for a pound of fruit." Jam cooking is like candymaking; it must be done over medium to high heat with great care to prevent scorching.

FOR JELLY: PREPARE JUICE; EXTRACT IT AND COOK WITH SUGAR. For maximum juice the fruit is first cooked soft in enough water to cover. Since squeezing produces a cloudy jelly, the preferred method of extracting is to let the pulp drip. Mother Wilder may have used a cloth bag hung from a cupboard door, but a standing colander will also do.

For cooking the juice with sugar the formula is the same as for jam: a scant pound of sugar for every pound or pint of liquid, depending on the sweetness of the fruit.

STERILIZE THE JARS. Laura was a mature adult by the time it was generally understood that food spoilage is the work of unseen bacteria, yeasts, and molds, and that these can be destroyed by "sterilizing." While this step is not exactly authentic, to omit it would be foolhardy.

To sterilize jars, wash them well and boil them in water to cover for 15 minutes, either in one large kettle or several smaller ones. Include lids, funnel, and utensils in the bath. Let them remain in hot water, removing as needed with sterile tongs.

TEST FOR DONENESS. Both jelly and jam must be cooked just the right amount. Too little cooking and the fruit will be runny; too much and it will become chewy. Nowadays we monitor the cooking with a candy thermometer and stop when it reaches 222°F. Our grandmothers used this "sheeting" test: Hold the coated stirring spoon horizontally over the pot. At first the syrup will drip from the edge. After enough cooking, the drips will unite and fall from the spoon in a thin sheet.

FILL THE STERILIZED JARS by ladling in the hot jam or jelly until almost full, using a wide-mouth funnel. The jars or glasses should be straight-sided for easy sealing, and they should be small, so they empty quickly. The refrigerator, it is true, will now keep large opened quantities from spoiling, but chilling dulls the flavor you have worked so hard to preserve.

SEAL THE JARS. The old custom was to cover the fruit with circles of letter paper soaked in brandy or brushed with egg white. Over this cover and the container edge another paper would be fastened with glue, or a moist animal bladder would be tied to shrink taut as it dried.

The decade of Laura's marriage brought with it the discovery of paraffin, a petroleum by-product that coats the contents like fat when heated and cools to a hard, airtight seal. It is applied in two thin layers—the first one on the hot contents, the second after the first has cooled. Follow package directions for use. Remember that it is flammable and also—when storing—that mice like to eat it.

LABEL AND STORE JARS PROPERLY. Don't trust your memory to tell you the contents and date of a jar after preserving season is over. An easy way to label is with a wax crayon directly on the still-warm jar. Light and heat will eventually affect the contents, so long-term storage in glass should be on cool covered shelves.

CRAB-APPLE JELLY

No guide to pioneer preserves can omit crab-apple jelly, one of the many adornments of the Wilder supper table. Just as the crab-apple tree was the parent of all apple trees, its fruit, with a natural abundance of pectin, was a common base for jellies made with other fruits. The delicate flavor can be amplified with a touch of lemon or subordinated to that of peaches, apricots, and berries.

We know that the "transcendent" variety was cultivated in Malone, but we like to think that Mother Wilder used the wild fruit of the American crab apple, a native of cool woods known for its fragrant pink blossoms. The sour hard fruits were found by the Indians to be sweeter in the spring if buried over the winter.

Nowadays there are many varieties of crab apples, some pale yellow and some deep crimson, some bearing in early summer and some in fall. Some have been cultivated as "ornamentals" with showy blossoms that produce only berrylike fruit. If you cannot find crab apples in the woods or a store, you may have to "forage" for them in well-landscaped neighborhoods.

For four 8-ounce jars of jelly you will need:
Crab apples, 4 pounds, stems removed
Granulated sugar, 3 cups
Lemon, juice of 1

Kettle, 8-quart; colander and stand; bowl, 3-quart; linen
    dishtowel; sterilizing kettle; 8-ounce preserve jars, 4; ladle,
    tongs, wide-mouth funnel; paraffin, 2 ounces; saucepan and
    tin cup for melting paraffin.

Read preserving steps, page 55.

Wash and halve crab apples, removing stems. Put them in the kettle with 8 cups of water, cover, and cook slowly until fruit is mushy (30 to 40 minutes). Some crab varieties will cook to a thick sauce; others will behave like grapes, remaining distinct from the liquid. In either case, you may ignore the rule against pressing out the juice.

Stand the colander over the bowl. Rinse the dishtowel in cold water, wring it out, and use it to line the colander. Ladle juice or sauce into the cloth, and press. Remove and discard spent pulp as necessary to make room for additional ladlings. Continue until kettle has been emptied of juice and pulp.

When all juice has been squeezed into bowl, measure it into kettle. Add water if necessary to make 4 cups in all. Begin sterilizing jars.

Heat juice to boiling and cook rapidly while stirring in sugar. After 15 minutes of cooking and stirring, begin testing for sheeting (page 57). The boiling surface of the liquid will become foamy as it approaches correct temperature, 222°F. If white scum forms, skim it off.

At first sign of sheeting, remove hot syrup from heat and stir in lemon juice. Ladle into sterilized jars. Seal jars with paraffin, label, date, and store in cool dark place.

PLUM PRESERVES

Can you believe that at a family supper, after downing ham, salt pork, baked beans, potatoes and gravy, bread and butter, turnips and pumpkin, the young Almanzo Wilder actually "ate plum preserves, and strawberry jam, and grape jelly, and spiced watermelon-rind pickles" and afterward "felt very comfortable inside"? Or could it be the imagination of a once-hungry storyteller?

Plum preserves would have been an attractive idea to an author who had picked many a wild fruit on the banks of Plum Creek but had known them only fresh with large stones or dried. This old recipe is clearly for wild plums, which must be cooked before the stones will come free. It will work just as well, however, with Damsons or other cultivated purple plums.

For four 8-ounce jars of preserves you will need:
Plums, $2\frac{1}{2}$ pounds wild or 2 pounds cultivated purple
Granulated sugar, 3 to $3\frac{1}{2}$ cups

Sterilizing kettle; 8-ounce preserve jars, 4; ladle, tongs, and
    wide-mouth funnel; kettle, 6-quart; paraffin, 2 ounces;
    saucepan and tin cup for melting paraffin

Read the preserving steps on page 55 and sterilize jars. In uncovered kettle simmer the plums in water to cover (about 1 quart) until they are tender and the skins split. This will take about 15 minutes. Skim off surface foam and let fruit cool.

Pour off the liquid and reserve. Remove stones from the fruit, pulling flesh and skin into small pieces as you do. Return 1 cup of liquid to the fruit in the kettle and add sugar—$3\frac{1}{2}$ cups for wild plums, less for cultivated ones. Cook mixture over medium heat until the syrup is "as thick as honey." This will take from 20 to 30 minutes. Test for sheeting.

Ladle cooked preserves into hot jars, seal with paraffin, label, date, and store in a cool dark place. Put leftover liquid in your vinegar jug (page 132).

HUSK-TOMATO PRESERVES

All day long while the girls were in school, Ma made preserves of the red tomatoes, of the purple husk-tomatoes, and of the golden ground-cherries.

LITTLE TOWN ON THE PRAIRIE

The terms "husk-tomato" and "ground-cherry" are often used for the same plant, but Laura Wilder drew a clear distinction. "The ground-cherries," she wrote, "grew on low leafy bushes. Thick on the stems under the large leaves hung the six-cornered bells, pale gray and thinner than paper, and inside each bell was a plump, golden, juicy round fruit.

"The husk-tomatoes were covered with a smooth, dull-brown husk. When this was opened there lay the round, bright-purple tomato, larger than a ground-cherry but much smaller than the red tomatoes that openly flaunted their bright colors."

Ground-cherries can still be found in the wild; our recipe is for husk-tomatoes because they are more generally available. Cultivated in the American Southwest as the tomatillo, they are a basic ingredient of chili dishes.

This recipe uses the old-fashioned practice of "resting" the preserves overnight, now explained in terms of chemical changes.

For 4 six-ounce jars of preserves you will need:
Husk-tomatoes, 2 pounds
Granulated sugar, 4 cups

Kettle, 6-quart; sterilizing kettle; 6-ounce preserve jars, 4;
    tongs, slotted spoon, ladle, wide-mouth funnel; paraffin, 2
    ounces; saucepan and tin cup for melting paraffin

Read preserving steps, page 55. Remove husks and rinse
tomatoes until stickiness is gone. Prepare a thick syrup by boiling
up the sugar in $\frac{1}{4}$ cup of water for about 10 minutes.

Add tomatoes to syrup and continue to boil, watching closely
and stirring frequently. When the fruit loses its bright color and
becomes transparent (after about 10 minutes), remove from heat,
cover, and let stand overnight. Most fruits will still be whole.

Next day sterilize the jars (page 56) and bring tomatoes and
syrup just to the boiling point. With slotted spoon remove tomatoes
to jars; with ladle and funnel add syrup to within $\frac{1}{2}$ inch of jar tops.
Seal with paraffin, label, date, and store in a cool dark place.

Serve the preserves as you would breakfast jam or as a relish
with pork roast, ham, or turkey.

STRAWBERRY JAM

*Wild strawberries were few that year, and late, because frost had
killed the first blossoms. Almanzo had to go far through the woods to
fill his pail full of the small, sweet, fragrant berries.*

FARMER BOY

Wild strawberries can still be found in the countryside, but
few people have the time and patience to pick enough for jam. The
fruits are small, low-growing, and often hidden under broad leaves;
the plants are a favorite hideout of chiggers. Wild strawberry jam
—any strawberry jam—should be eaten with a proper respect for
those who gathered the fruit.

This recipe is geared to commercially grown strawberries, which are sold by the dry pint, weighing about twelve ounces, and which will reduce somewhat in weight after hulling and sorting.

For four 6-ounce jars of jam you will need:
Strawberries, 3 dry pints
Granulated sugar, $2\frac{1}{2}$ cups

Kettle, 3-quart; sterilizing kettle; 6-ounce preserve jars, 4; ladle,
    tongs, wide-mouth funnel; saucepan and tin cup for
    melting paraffin, paraffin, 2 ounces

Read preserving steps, page 55. Wash strawberries and re-move the hulls and leaves. Slice them, cutting out all soft spots.

Put sugar and sliced berries in the 3-quart kettle in alternating layers, beginning and ending with sugar. Cover and set aside until all the sugar is absorbed in the juice. This will take about 3 hours.

Wash and sterilize the jars. Bring berries and sugar to a boil over high heat. Reduce heat to medium and continue to cook about 20 minutes, stirring frequently. Stop cooking when the syrup sheets. Ladle jam into jars using funnel, seal with paraffin, label, and date.

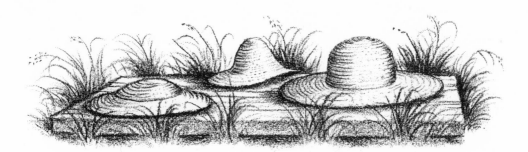

Chapter
5

Foods from Tilled Fields

WHEAT. How important it was in Laura's life! From the time the Ingallses left the Big Woods of Wisconsin their fortunes were shaped by the quest for a good wheat crop. In each new home—on the Kansas prairie, in Minnesota, and on the South Dakota claim— Pa found open land covered with tough grass. He broke this sod, plowed the earth, and planted the wheat that was to be his money crop. "When that crop was harvested, Pa said, they'd be out of debt and have more money than they knew what to do with. He'd have a buggy, Ma would have a silk dress, they'd all have new shoes and eat beef every Sunday."

But it was not to be. Thanks to border disputes, grasshoppers, weeds, blackbirds, and drought, the Ingallses harvested more grief than grain. When Laura hesitated about marrying a farmer, Almanzo promised her "fifty acres of wheat this year . . . and another fifty acres next spring." Then hail and drought claimed *their* harvests, and the young Wilders finally turned their backs on wheat and headed for the "land of the big apple," Missouri.

Why wheat? Because wheat yields flour for bread, the "staff of life." Because a war-torn Europe was hungry for American wheat, and a new railroad spanning the continent had opened a way to ship it to eastern ports. Because the prairie seemed to offer everything

wheat needed to prosper—open fields, warm summers, enough rain. Because one man with a team could be expected to raise enough wheat to keep his family in flour, to pay shares to threshers, and to sell for life's necessities and a few luxuries.

"Think, Caroline—this level, rich land, not a stone or stump to contend with, and only three miles from a railroad! We can sell every grain of wheat we raise!"

Pa's dream eventually came true, though not for his own family. The prairie that the pioneers broke and the homesteaders tamed has become the largest wheat-producing area in the world, furnishing grain to countries around the globe. It is we who enjoy the fruits of Pa's labors.

Great as it is, the United States' wheat crop is second to another crop. Our corn harvest is roughly twice that of wheat, but most corn stays on the farm, feeding hogs, cows, and beef cattle. Corn dishes in one form or another appear throughout this book, and we include some here because corn was an important field crop to Ingallses and Wilders both. The same crop that fed their livestock and furnished their hominy was eaten green at the table. Sweet corn was known to the Indians and colonial Americans, but not until our century was it specially bred and widely cultivated for human consumption.

Buckwheat was another field crop, although it isn't really a grain. It does have a seed that is ground into a very flavorful flour plus qualities that suited it to northern frontier farms: buckwheat flourishes in poor, scarcely tilled soil and has a short growing season. With relatively little effort frontiersmen could sow a crop in June and reap it in early September. Quick hotcakes of buckwheat flour were ideal fare for miners, railroaders, and others like the Wilder brothers who lacked the time and ingredients to make light bread.

Breadmaking, Then and Now

Only three ingredients are essential to raised bread—flour, liquid, and leavening. These, plus salt, are still the only ones used by small bakeries in Europe, where many people buy their bread daily.

Without nearby bakeries to supply them, colonial and pioneer housewives took on, with many other challenges, the task of breadbaking. Home breadbaking became an American tradition, and bread recipes became a distinguishing feature of American cookbooks.

Keeping a wood-fired oven, whether in chimney or cookstove, hot enough for baking was not practical on a daily basis, so baking became a once-a-week custom. With weekly baking came a product different from bakery bread, a "keeping" loaf. To produce it the housewife included in her dough ingredients that would retard its staling and that would offset variations in flour quality, in homemade yeasts, and in oven temperatures. Although it is fashionable to blame twentieth-century commercial bakers, the soft, long-lasting loaf with fat and sugar is out of our own home-baking tradition.

BREAD FLOUR. The wheat flour used by Ma Ingalls and Mother Wilder was ground between buhrstones, then sifted or "bolted" to separate the fine white powder from the coarser hulls, or bran, and the germ. Whole-wheat or graham flour was unbolted. Mother Wilder and Ma preferred white flour because it lacks germ oil that can sour and because it produces baked goods light in texture and color. But most of the time Ma used a less refined, less expensive middle grade, flecked with brown bran.

Today white flour comes to us from high-speed mills where the germ and bran are removed from the grain as a first step. It is our "all-purpose" everyday flour; for us, whole wheat is something special. White flour actually starts as a yellowish powder that lightens with time. Bleaching agents are often used to speed up the process. We specify "unbleached" flour here because it seems to be more hospitable to wild yeasts.

Other flours—rye, buckwheat, and cornmeal—were and are used in yeast bread, but rarely alone. Wheat is the only flour that produces sufficient gluten, the stretchy protein cells that capture the gas released by active yeast.

YEAST is a live plant that needs warmth, moisture, and food to grow. It is the feeding process, called fermentation, that changes flour-and-water paste into stretchy, puffy bread dough. Colonial housewives bought yeast at the brewery or bakery or concocted it at home from hops, potatoes, and molasses. When Ma Ingalls was near a store, she was able to buy packaged cultivated yeast cakes; when she was not, she relied on her own sour dough, a "wild" yeast. Today yeast is generally sold in two sizes of cakes—.6 ounce and 2 ounces—as well as in $\frac{1}{4}$-ounce envelopes of dry granules. The small cake and the envelope contents are equal in leavening power; they are roughly equal to $\frac{1}{4}$ of a 2-ounce cake.

As LIQUID for bread, water will do, but milk produces a tenderer texture. Milk used for bread in Laura's day had first to be scalded to eliminate yeast-killing acids. Today pasteurization does that job for us, but the liquid temperature is still important. It must be warm enough to nurture the yeast, yet not hot enough to kill it.

The ideal is body temperature, 98°F, which we call "lukewarm" and Laura called "bloodwarm" or "milkwarm."

SUGAR was often added to bread because it speeds the action of yeast. Expensive white sugar was used in small quantities with white flour. Whole wheat flour offers less nourishment for yeast, and molasses—being cheaper—was often added in amounts we would find cloying today. Sugar also helps loaves to brown nicely in home ovens.

SALT checks the action of yeast, so it was used sparingly before the days of reliable commercial yeasts. A teaspoonful to three loaves was typical in Laura's youth. Today, with many bread recipes calling for nine times that amount, her bread would taste quite flat. Our recipes reflect a compromise of one teaspoon of salt per loaf.

FAT in the form of lard, drippings, or butter was favored for once-a-week baking because it keeps bread tender and moist. Liquid and solid vegetable fats for baking are a modern development.

BREADMAKING STEPS, THEN AND NOW

Making the yeast breads in this chapter involves some or all of the following steps:

PREPARE THE YEAST. Yeast must have moisture and warmth to come alive. Cake and powdered yeasts keep well when dry and cool, but they must be soaked in warm liquid for breadmaking.

MIX INGREDIENTS WELL. Oldtimers formed a well in the center of the flour supply, poured in other ingredients, and mixed until the dough felt right. Modern style is to beat flour into the liquid gradually, often with an electric beater.

KNEAD THE DOUGH. Beating is replaced by kneading when the dough becomes heavy. This can now be done by a machine with a dough hook, but the old-fashioned way is more rewarding. To knead by hand without tiring you must "get your back into it," working with arms straight down on a surface at thigh level. At a modern kitchen counter you might need to stand on a footstool. Dust the surface with flour and drop the dough in the center. Sink the heels of your hands into the middle. Push away from your body, then fold the dough back toward you. Give the mass a clockwise quarter-turn like a wheel and repeat. As you knead add flour bit by bit until the dough stops absorbing and is no longer sticky. Knead this way for at least five minutes until the dough feels like your cheek. If you stop sooner the bread will have a coarse texture and will slump on the pan.

SET THE DOUGH TO RISE. This is where Nature takes over and yeast action makes the dough expand. Grease the dough ball to keep it from drying out, put it in a bowl, cover with a towel, and stand it in a warm place (75 to 100°F). In a pioneer kitchen there was always a warm place on or near the cookstove. A modern gas stove pilot light will do, or an electric oven with only the light bulb on. Or try putting the bowl on a sunny window sill or in a pan of hot water.

PUNCH AND SHAPE THE DOUGH. When the dough has doubled in size, take it out of the bowl, knock it flat with a good punch, and stretch it out on the board. A knife is best for dividing into loaf units. How you shape each loaf has much to do with its final quality. Loaf pans are the easiest way, but Ma didn't have them. She may have stretched the dough into a rectangle and rolled it, jelly-roll style, for an oblong loaf. Or she may have mounded it for a round loaf.

SET THE LOAVES TO RISE. Repeat steps for first rising.

BAKE THE LOAVES in a preheated oven. How long and how hot depends on the recipe. Ma would have begun her baking day by building up the fire with just the right number and kind of logs. She knew that a loaf is finished when it holds its shape, is nicely browned, and sounds hollow when tapped.

COOL THE LOAVES, but never on a wood surface, the old caution ran. A clean cloth was used then; racks are now more common. Hot bread will pull apart if you try to cut it and will get tough if you wrap it, so give it time and air before serving or storing.

SERVE YOUR BREAD with the same care you took in making it, whether you offer it with a meal, as a snack, or in a sandwich.

LIGHT BREAD

> ". . . tomorrow we'll finish unpacking and be finally settled. I must do a baking too. It's a blessing to have yeast once more. I feel as though I never want to see another sour-dough biscuit."
>
> "Your light bread is good and so are your sour-dough biscuits," Pa told her. "But we won't have either if I don't rustle something to bake them with. Tomorrow I'll haul a load of wood from Lake Henry."
>
> BY THE SHORES OF SILVER LAKE

Light bread is another name for white-flour yeast bread. Instead of combining all ingredients to start, Ma made what we call a sponge, allowing the yeast to work with *part* of the liquid and flour. This sponge method enabled early cooks to make sure their yeasts were working (proof them) without risking all the flour and to produce a ripe dough that would hold shape without loaf pans.

In cool weather Ma made or "set" the sponge the night before baking day, leaving it to work at room temperature (hers was between 45° and 60°F). In summer she would have done it very early in the morning. Because of fast-acting yeast and heated kitchens we must refrigerate an overnight sponge.

For three 1¼-pound loaves you will need:
Yeast, 2 small cakes or envelopes
White flour, up to 10 cups unbleached all-purpose
Homogenized milk, 1 cup
Drippings, 3 tablespoons for dough, 2 teaspoons for pans

Salt, 1 tablespoon
Granulated sugar, 1 tablespoon

Bowl, 3-quart; dinner plates, 2; bowl, 5-quart; breadboard;
   dishtowel; baking sheets, 2

Read "Breadmaking Steps," page 68. The night before baking day, crumble yeast into 1 cup of bloodwarm water in smaller bowl and let soak a few minutes. Add another cup of bloodwarm water and 4 cups of flour. Beat until it becomes too difficult. Cover bowl with a plate, rest it on a second plate (to catch spills), and refrigerate overnight.

Next morning set out the sponge, milk, and drippings to warm up while you breakfast (or heat the milk with 3 tablespoons of drippings until drippings melt in it).

In the larger bowl mix milk, salt, sugar, 3 tablespoons of drippings, and 1 cup of flour. Stir in the yeast sponge. Add 2 cups more flour and beat, then 1 more cup. Use a chopping motion when beating becomes difficult.

When dough pulls away from bowl turn it onto the floured breadboard, scraping the bowl clean. Knead dough for about 3 minutes; rest for 3. Continue alternating for at least 15 minutes, adding more flour whenever dough becomes sticky. It may absorb up to another cup of flour.

With remaining drippings, grease larger bowl and baking sheets. Put the dough in the bowl, turning it to grease it as you do, and set it to rise under a lid or dishtowel. If the climate is dry moisten the towel.

When dough has doubled in size, about $1\frac{1}{2}$ hours later, punch it down. Remove to breadboard and pull it into a rope. With a knife cut dough in three equal pieces. Save one segment, if you wish, for Light Biscuits (following recipe). Shape the others into loaves and place them well apart on a baking sheet for $1\frac{1}{2}$ to 2 hours, until nicely expanded. Preheat the oven to 350°F and bake the loaves for 30 minutes. Remove the loaves from the baking sheet, place them on oven rack, and bake another 10 to 15 minutes. Cool the loaves thoroughly before slicing.

LIGHT BISCUITS

The bread-sponge was lifting the lid of the pan. Ma hurriedly floured the breadboard, and kneaded the dough. Then she got dinner. She was putting the pan of light biscuits in the oven when Pa came driving the wagon up the hill. Behind him the wagon box was piled high with willow brush that he had brought for summer fuel, for there were no real trees at Lake Henry.

BY THE SHORES OF SILVER LAKE

Busy pioneers made Saturday's dough in large quantities and used it for baked goods besides bread. With the addition of more fat, sugar, and an egg, and with different shaping, light bread dough became light-as-a-cloud biscuits, just in time for noon dinner. Today we would call them dinner rolls, reserving the term "biscuit" for a quick bread made with baking powder.

Small biscuits were always considered best. If there wasn't a wineglass on hand a small empty tin like our modern tomato-paste can served as a cutter.

For 20 to 24 biscuits $2\frac{1}{4}$ inches round you will need:
Egg, 1
Dough for Light Bread ($\frac{1}{3}$ of preceding recipe), $1\frac{1}{4}$ pounds or
    enough for 1 loaf
Granulated sugar, 1 tablespoon
Butter, lard, or drippings, 2 tablespoons
White flour, unbleached all-purpose, for dusting

Bowl, 2-quart; dripping pan, 11-by-15-inch; breadboard and
    rolling pin; cutter, 2- to $2\frac{1}{4}$-inch; dishtowel

Beat the egg in the bowl and stir in dough a pinch at a time. Add sugar. Melt fat in dripping pan, coat pan, and pour surplus into dough. Beat all until the slippery globs of dough change into a stiff dough ball. This will take 5 minutes of hard work; you may wish to work seated with the bowl between your knees.

Dust dough with flour and turn onto floured breadboard. Pat

it into a thick ($\frac{3}{8}$-inch) blanket, and smooth it out with a few light strokes of a floured rolling pin.

Cut out rounds, dipping cutter in flour after each use. (Dough scraps become tough when rerolled, but they can be soaked in a cup of water to make sponge for another batch.) Place the biscuits side by side on the greased pan. Cover with dishtowel and set to rise on warm (75° to 95°F) stove.

After about an hour, when biscuits are puffy, preheat oven to 350°F. Turn it to 400° as you put in the pan. Bake about 15 minutes, until biscuits are lightly browned. Watch closely; a few minutes' overbaking can turn clouds into golfballs! Serve warm in a cloth-lined bowl.

WHITE-FLOUR DUMPLINGS (SOUR-MILK BISCUITS)

> *Thanksgiving dinner was good. Pa had shot a wild goose for it. Ma had to stew the goose because there was no fireplace, and no oven in the little stove. But she made dumplings in the gravy.*
>
> ON THE BANKS OF PLUM CREEK

That was in the dugout in Plum Creek. In Kansas, stewed jack rabbit "with white-flour dumplings and plenty of gravy" made a special meal for Mr. Edwards.

Dumplings are dough cooked in liquid. Almost every nationality has its version, some made with eggs and cream. Ma's dumplings were nothing more than wet biscuits—not the light yeast kind or the sour-dough kind, but the kind Mrs. Boast knew best, made with sour milk. Also known as soda biscuits, they are puffed up by gas released when acid milk acts on baking soda. With the invention of a single powder combining acid and soda they have become baking-powder biscuits.

Dumplings are easy to make. Biscuits, however, require rolling out, and too much handling and too much flour make them tough. Don't be discouraged if your first batch is heavy; developing a light touch takes practice. Always mix the soda well into the flour to start; otherwise it will leave telltale rust streaks in the finished product.

This recipe will produce more than enough dumplings to cover a 10-inch bake-oven or about two dozen small biscuits. Cultured buttermilk is recommended as the modern equivalent to sour raw milk.

For six servings you will need:
White flour, 2 cups unbleached all-purpose
Salt, 1 heaping teaspoon
Baking soda, 1 teaspoon
Cultured buttermilk, $\frac{3}{4}$ to 1 cup

Bowl, 2-quart

DUMPLINGS ONLY

Cooked stew or 2 cups broth

Bake-oven or skillet, 10-inch

BISCUITS ONLY

Drippings, 3 tablespoons

Dripping pan or baking sheet; pastry board and rolling pin;
    2-inch can, wineglass, or other cutter

FOR DUMPLINGS

Have a kettle of stew or a skillet of broth simmering on the stove. In the bowl mix dry ingredients well. Pour in $\frac{3}{4}$ cup of the buttermilk and mix quickly with a fork. Your dough should be stiff but too moist for rolling; add remaining milk if needed.

With a soupspoon drop the dough onto the bubbling liquid, covering the surface. Let simmer on medium-low heat until dumplings puff and lose their gloss (8 to 10 minutes). Cover with a lid, reduce heat to low, and simmer another 8 to 10 minutes, until dumplings are cooked through. Dumplings in a skillet can be cooked uncovered by turning them halfway through.

FOR BISCUITS

Preheat oven to 425°F. Use oven to melt drippings in pan or baking sheet. In the bowl mix dry ingredients well. Turn pan to coat it with fat, then pour drippings into bowl and work into flour mixture with fork or fingers. Add buttermilk and mix quickly to make a ball of dough. If too dry to blend well add more milk, a spoonful at a time.

Dust pastry board with flour and press out dough on it. Roll lightly to a thickness of $\frac{3}{8}$ inch. Dip cutter edge in flour and cut out rounds of dough with as little waste as possible. (Scraps can be baked for snacks, thrown in boiling soup for dumplings, or put with sour-dough starter.)

Arrange biscuits side by side on pan, inverting them after placing to grease tops as well as bottoms. Bake in upper half of oven for 12 minutes. Break open a sample; if not cooked through, bake another 5 minutes. Use a hotpad to remove hot biscuits to a napkin-lined bowl and serve immediately.

SALT-RISING BREAD

This fine-grained bread with a cheesy flavor was part of the Ingallses' Christmas feasts in the Big Woods and on the Kansas prairie. Like the sour-dough baked goods in the following recipes, salt-rising bread starts with a "natural" ferment, but this one works at a higher temperature than sour dough and cannot be extended by doubling.

Salt-rising bread is made in three stages—a ferment, a sponge, and a dough, all of which require sustained warmth in the range of 110° to 130°F. That's why it is hard to make in a kitchen that has no banked fire, chimney corner, or kerosene lamp. Lacking a gas pilot light or an oven lamp with control switch, we found two good alternative sources of warmth for the 20-hour ferment. One is a draftsman's lamp with a 60-watt bulb that can be lowered over the container. Even better for energy saving is a quart vacuum bottle that uses retained heat.

You may divide the dough in two loaves and bake them in smaller, separate casseroles. If you use an uncovered baking sheet, you won't get as handsome and round a loaf as a covered kettle produces.

For one 2½-pound loaf you will need:
Homogenized milk, 1 cup
Salt, 2 teaspoons
Brown sugar, 2 tablespoons
Cornmeal, 4 tablespoons stoneground white or yellow
White flour, 6 cups all-purpose unbleached
Drippings, 2 to 4 tablespoons

Vacuum bottle, 1-quart, wide-mouth; saucepan, 1-quart; bowl, 3-quart; bake-oven, 4-quart, or 2 smaller casseroles with lids; additional pans for hot water

Start the ferment at noon of the day before baking. Preheat the vacuum bottle with boiling water. Heat milk in saucepan just to the boiling point. Remove pan from stove and stir into the milk half the salt, half the brown sugar, and all the cornmeal. Next stir in $\frac{1}{2}$ cup of flour. Empty the warm bottle and pour in the lumpy milk batter. Fasten the lid loosely and let the bottle stand, undisturbed, on a kitchen counter.

Next morning after breakfast take a sample of the ferment with a long-handled teaspoon, opening and closing the bottle quickly. If the sample is foamy, like a milkshake, it is ready to use. If it is unchanged after another test, at noon, abandon it and try another day.

In the bowl prepare the sponge by mixing 1 cup of hot tap water, 1 teaspoon of salt, 1 tablespoon of brown sugar, and 2 table-spoons of drippings. Mix well, then stir in 2 cups of flour and beat to a stiff batter. Add the ferment from the bottle and beat it in well. Cover the bowl with a plate and set it in a pan of hot tap water.

The sponge is ready for doughmaking when it is very smelly and puffy. This may take 1 to 2 hours and require a change of water bath to maintain warmth.

Into the sponge beat 2 cups of flour for a stiff dough. Work in another cup or more of flour with the hands, alternating kneading and resting for about 10 minutes. Grease the bake-oven or casseroles and lid(s) with drippings. Shape the dough in a ball (or two balls) and place in the bake-oven or casseroles, turning dough as you do to grease it all over. Cover with lid and set in a pan or basin of hot tap water. The loaf should expand to about half again its bulk. This may take up to 3 hours and require changes of the water bath to maintain warmth.

Bake the risen dough in the covered bake-oven or casseroles in a stove oven preheated to 350°F. After 30 minutes remove the lid and bake about 15 minutes longer. The loaf is fully baked when it is evenly browned on top. When completely cooled it can be cut in slices as thin as $\frac{1}{4}$ inch.

SOUR-DOUGH STARTER

> *"But how do you make the sour dough?" Mrs. Boast asked.*
>
> *"You start it," said Ma, "by putting some flour and warm water in a jar and letting it stand till it sours."*
>
> *"Then when you use it, always leave a little," said Laura. "And put in the scraps of biscuit dough, like this, and more warm water," Laura put in the warm water, "and cover it," she put the clean cloth and the plate on the jar, "and just set it in a warm place," she set it in its place on the shelf by the stove. "And it's always ready to use, whenever you want it."*
>
> BY THE SHORES OF SILVER LAKE

A sour-dough starter is a leaven that develops from microscopic wild yeast and bacteria present in the air. Its usual form is a batter; for traveling it was worked dry with flour and stuffed in the flour sack.

Home bakers who were far from yeast supplies used sour dough to raise bread, biscuits, and pancakes, longing all the while for the makings of a "sweet loaf." Today, when the sweet loaf is everywhere, the tart flavor and distinctive texture of sour-dough bread are highly prized, and loaves are flown all over the world from commercial sour-dough bakeries in San Francisco.

Laura makes beginning a starter sound very easy, but it is not. She had patience, experience, favorable climate, and the warmth of a "shelf by the stove." If you want to make a starter exactly as she did, without such helps as sugar, yeast, or milk, you may have to try several times. When you succeed you will understand why gold prospectors in Alaska so cherished their starters that they became known as "sourdoughs." If you want to make sour-dough bread as well as biscuits (following recipe), you can find many recipes at your local library and at natural-foods stores.

> *To begin a starter you will need:*
> White flour, $1\frac{1}{4}$ cups unbleached all-purpose
> Water, 1 cup bloodwarm (see below)
> Glass jar, 1-quart, with lid or piece of cheesecloth; saucer;
>   rubber band; bowl, 1-quart

Mix flour and water in the jar and let stand until the batter bubbles and rises. This may take anywhere from overnight to a week! Success will depend on several factors:

WATER QUALITY. Chemically-treated city water may be hostile to wild yeast. If your efforts with city tap water fail, try using bottled spring water.

TEMPERATURE. The batter must be warm but not hot, between 80° and 95°F. In cool weather place the jar in an oven warmed only by a 60-watt light bulb, under a hanging 60-watt lamp, or near the furnace.

HUMIDITY. Since yeast needs moisture to live, sour dough is hard to start in dry desert climates. What's more, the amount of moisture in the air seems to affect the final product. A starter from foggy San Francisco might produce a quick-rising dough with a coarse, airy texture, while one in sunny San Jose 50 miles away might result in a slow-rising dense dough. The same kitchen can produce different starters on different days.

OBSERVATION. When you mix the starter notice the feel and aroma, for later comparison. A rubber band around the jar at the starter level will help you note any rising.

COVERING. A loose lid or covering of damp cheesecloth will keep out insects and prevent drying of the starter. A jar under a hanging bulb should not have a cover.

STIRRING. Stir only if liquid rises to the top.

Bubbles in the dough and expanded volume, or rising, are the chief signs that the starter is "alive" and working. The aroma should be pleasantly sour, the texture tacky. If after several days the batter has developed only a bad smell, throw it out, scald the jar, and start again.

A new starter needs to ripen before it is ready to use. It must also be fed to keep from dying. In the bowl mix up another flour and water batter and stir in the live starter. This is called "doubling." Leave the mixture in a warm place for several hours until it is bubbly. Return half to the jar and give the rest to a friend.

Store the starter in the refrigerator for a few days to ripen. After that it will be ready for doubling again and to use for biscuits (following recipe) or for other breads of your choice.

SOUR-DOUGH BISCUITS

> *"When you haven't milk enough to have sour milk, however do you make such delicious biscuits, Laura?" she asked.*
> *"Why, you just use sour dough," Laura said.*
> *Mrs. Boast had never made sour-dough biscuits! It was fun to show her. Laura measured out the cups of sour dough, put in the soda and salt and flour, and rolled out the biscuits on the board.*

> BY THE SHORES OF SILVER LAKE

No wonder Laura was surprised at Mrs. Boast that Christmas morning! Biscuits were second only to bread in importance on the Ingalls table, and more often than not they were made with a sour-dough, rather than a sour-milk, leaven. Both sours serve the same purpose here—to react with the soda and release a gas that puffs up the dough.

The Christmas Eve biscuits had been oven-baked, but on Christmas day, with a rabbit roast and johnny-cake in the oven, we think Laura may have used a method we find better—skillet baking.

The Ingallses were able to make these biscuits quickly because their sour dough was always warm and "working." This recipe assumes that your starter comes from the refrigerator, and must be "doubled" and allowed to warm before baking.

For 24 to 30 biscuits you will need:
Sour-Dough Starter, 1 cup (page 77)
White flour, $4\frac{1}{2}$ cups unbleached all-purpose
Salt, 1 teaspoon
Baking soda, 1 teaspoon
Drippings, 2 teaspoons

Bowls, 3-quart, 2; rolling pin and breadboard; cutter, $2\frac{1}{4}$-inch—
    can or wineglass; baking sheet; skillet, 10- to 12-inch

At least 4 hours before baking extend the starter by stirring it in a bowl with $2\frac{1}{2}$ cups of flour and 2 cups of bloodwarm water. Cover and let stand at 75° to 80°F.

When the mixture is bubbling, remove a cup of it to the

refrigerator jar for future use. In a second bowl mix well the remaining flour (2 cups), the salt, and baking soda (soda will leave telltale rust streaks if not sufficiently mixed!). Stir in the bubbling sour batter until all ingredients are blended and moist.

With floured hands press the dough flat on a floured breadboard. Roll it lightly to a thickness of $\frac{1}{2}$ inch. With floured cutter stamp out as many biscuits as possible. Put leftover scraps with the refrigerated starter.

If you have the time, a half-hour's rising on a greased baking sheet will improve the biscuits' shape. If not, proceed to grease the skillet with drippings and heat it to medium-low. Put in as many biscuits as will fit. Cook 10 minutes; turn and cook 10 minutes more. Remove hot biscuits to a napkin-lined dish and proceed to cook remaining biscuits. Watch temperature; if it is too high the biscuits will develop a thick crust.

GRAHAM BREAD

"Brown, nutty-tasting graham bread" was one of several breads served at the church's "New England Supper" in *Little Town on the Prairie*. Whole-wheat or "unbolted" flour had taken on the name of Sylvester Graham, a minister who thirty years before Laura's birth advocated such novel health measures as sleeping with windows open, eliminating tight corsets and neckties, and eating whole-grain bread.

Graham bread was often made from the sponge for Light Bread (see page 70) by adding whole-wheat rather than white flour in the morning. This recipe uses instead the now popular "straight" method, combining all ingredients at the start. It includes some white flour; a bread of only stoneground whole wheat is heavy, dense, and crumbly (see "Long Winter" Bread, next recipe). Notice that the dough is a moist one requiring no kneading.

Whole-grain breads are slow to rise. Allow six hours from start to serving.

For two 1½-pound loaves you will need:
Yeast, 2 small cakes or envelopes
Whole-wheat flour, 4 cups stoneground
White flour, 2 cups unbleached all-purpose
Salt, 2 teaspoons
Molasses, ¼ cup
Drippings, 1 tablespoon

Bowl, 1½-quart; bowl, 3-quart; dishtowel; breadboard; deep
     baking pans or loaf pans, 2

In the smaller bowl crumble yeast into ¼ cup bloodwarm
water. Let soak 5 minutes.

Meanwhile in large bowl combine flours and salt, and make
a wide, deep well in the center.

To the yeast add molasses and 2 cups of bloodwarm water
and stir. Pour this liquid into the well and stir around and around
at the center. Gradually the batter will thicken into a stiff dough.
When all flour is mixed in, dust the dough mass with an extra
handful of flour so it no longer sticks to the bowl. Cover with
dishtowel and set it to rise at room temperature (68°F) for about 2
hours, until doubled in bulk.

With a floured fist punch the dough down and turn it onto
a floured board. Knead a few times, then pull into a rope and cut
in half with a knife. Flatten each half into a rectangle and roll up like
a jelly roll. Grease loaf pans with drippings. Turn loaves to grease
them as you put them in pans. Cover, and set to rise for another 2
hours.

Preheat oven to 350°F. Bake the loaves about 40 minutes,
then remove bread from pans. Return loaves to oven rack to bake
10 minutes more. Cool well. Slicing will be easiest next day.

"LONG WINTER" BREAD

"I wish you'd help me, anyway, Charles," Ma said. She took the coffee mill from Mary and emptied the ground wheat from its little drawer. She filled the small hopper with kernels and handed the mill to Pa. "I'll need another grinding to make the bread for dinner," she told him.

Ma took the covered dish of souring from its warm place under the stove. She stirred it briskly, then measured two cupfuls into a pan, added salt and saleratus, and the flour that Mary and Carrie had ground. Then she took the mill from Pa and added the flour he had made.

THE LONG WINTER

Thus the author describes the making of the daily loaf that kept her family from starvation during the winter of 1880. "It had a fresh nutty flavor," she said, "that seemed almost to take the place of butter."

You are not likely to find this heavy, coarse loaf as satisfying as Laura did—unless you eat nothing else during the day, help to grind the grain, and share it with five hungry people in a room where a bottle of ink might freeze.

For a six-portion loaf you will need:
White flour, $2\frac{1}{2}$ cups unbleached all-purpose
Sour-Dough Starter, 1 cup (page 77)
Dried bread, several slices
Wheat berries, 1 pound
Salt, 2 teaspoons
Baking soda, 1 teaspoon
Drippings, 1 teaspoon

Coffee grinder, hand-powered; bowl, 3-quart; pie pan or milk pan, 9 to 10 inches

Because Ma's recipe calls for "two cupfuls" of starter, you must start several hours in advance by extending your sourdough

supply. Using all-purpose flour to keep the starter "clear," mix $2\frac{1}{2}$ cups of the flour with 2 cups bloodwarm water and the starter. Cover and let stand in a warm place until bubbly.

Clear the grinder of coffee by grinding the dry bread (washing might result in rust). Dispose of all crumbs. Grind the berries as fine as possible. One pound of berries should produce about $3\frac{1}{2}$ cups of flour.

Ma appears to have mixed her dough directly in the baking pan—one well-seasoned enough to do without grease. For novices we suggest a mixing bowl and greased pan.

In the bowl mix 2 cups of starter you have just extended, salt, soda, and 3 cups of hand-ground flour. When stirring becomes too difficult, use your hand and knead the dough in the bowl for a few minutes. Use more flour to prevent sticking.

Return remaining starter to refrigerator. Shape dough into a round loaf and place in greased round pan. With a knife score lines for six wedge-shaped portions. Cover with a cloth and let rise for 30 minutes.

Preheat oven to 350°F and bake loaf for about 45 minutes. Cool before dividing along lines.

RYE'N'INJUN

> *In the pantry Mother was filling the six-quart pan with boiled beans . . . . Then Almanzo saw her open the flour barrels. She flung rye flour and cornmeal into the big yellow crock, and stirred in milk and eggs and things, and poured the big baking-pan full of the yellow-gray rye'n'injun dough.*
>
> *"You fetch the rye'n'injun, Almanzo; don't spill it," she said. She snatched up the pan of beans and Almanzo followed more slowly with the heavy pan of rye'n'injun. Father opened the big doors of the oven in the heater, and Mother slid the beans and the bread inside. They would slowly bake there, till Sunday dinner-time.*
>
> FARMER BOY

Nowadays we would call this Boston Brown Bread, using all-purpose flour instead of rye, adding raisins, and "steaming" instead of slow-oven baking. Its history reaches back to the first New England colonists, whose only grains were the rye they brought from Europe and the corn they got from the Indians (hence "injun" for cornmeal). Later wheat flour was added and the name "thirded bread" was used for the three grains.

How and why this loaf changed over the years from an unsweetened yeast bread to a soda bread heavy with molasses we do not know, but it happened before Mother Wilder raised her family. Our recipe calls for slow overnight baking as she did it, but to conserve energy you can get the same results by "steaming," cooking in a closed container set in a boiling water bath for three or four hours. Consult any American cookbook or your electric slow cooker directions.

For six ample servings you will need:
Drippings for greasing
Cornmeal, 1½ cups yellow stoneground
Rye flour, 1½ cups
Baking soda, 2 teaspoons
Salt, 1 teaspoon
Eggs, 2
Cultured buttermilk, 1 cup
Dark molasses, ¾ cup

Baking pans, two 9-by-13-inch; bowl, 1-gallon; bowl, 2-quart; baking sheet

Arrange two racks in the oven. On the lower one place one of the baking pans and fill it with hot tap water (a source of moisture replacing Mother Wilder's baked beans). Preheat the oven to 200°F. Generously grease the other pan with drippings.

In the larger bowl mix well the cornmeal, rye flour, soda, and salt. In the smaller bowl beat the eggs; stir in the buttermilk, then the molasses. Pour liquid into dry ingredients and stir just until they are moistened. Do not beat. Pour batter into greased pan and smooth out. Cover with a baking sheet. Place on the upper oven rack directly above the water. Bake for about 12 hours (it will be ready to eat after 4 hours, but oldtimers seemed to feel "the longer the better").

DOUGHNUTS

That night was Saturday night. All day long Mother had been baking, and when Almanzo went into the kitchen for the milkpails, she was still frying doughnuts. The place was full of their hot, brown smell. . . .

Almanzo took the biggest doughnut from the pan and bit off its crisp end. Mother was rolling out the golden dough, slashing it into long strips, rolling and doubling and twisting the strips. Her fingers flew; you could hardly see them. The strips seemed to twist themselves under her hands, and to leap into the big copper kettle of swirling hot fat.

Plump! they went to the bottom, sending up bubbles. Then quickly they came popping up, to float and slowly swell, till they rolled themselves over, their pale golden backs going into the fat and their plump brown bellies rising out of it.

They rolled over, Mother said, because they were twisted. Some women made a new-fangled shape, round, with a hole in the middle. But round doughnuts wouldn't turn themselves over. Mother didn't have time to waste turning doughnuts; it was quicker to twist them.

FARMER BOY

It seemed likely to us that Mother Wilder would make raised doughnuts, using some of the yeast dough from Saturday's baking. But near Malone, New York, where Mother Wilder grew up, married, and had her children, we learned that "raised doughnuts are cut in circles; plain doughnuts are twisted." With a bow to local tradition, we pass along this recipe from the *Malone Cook Book* of 1898 for plain doughnuts that are quick and easy to make and very good.

Pure lard, unlike water, which boils away at 212°F, can become very hot. It is wise to take precautions against burning yourself and the food. Don't work alone, but do concentrate. Wear an apron; have hotpads handy; keep space next to the kettle clear in case it must be moved from the burner. Use a candy thermometer to monitor fat temperature, and don't let it go over 400°F. Use dry utensils; water and hot fat are an explosive mixture. If you must turn away from the fat kettle, to answer the doorbell or such, remove the kettle from the heat first.

For 2 dozen doughnuts you will need:
Lard, 2 pounds
Egg, 1
Baking soda, 1 teaspoon
Salt, $\frac{1}{2}$ teaspoon
Sour cream, 1 cup
White flour, $2\frac{1}{4}$ cups unbleached all-purpose
Powdered sugar, a shaker full

Kettle, 3-quart; bowl, 2-quart; rolling pin; candy thermometer

Melt lard in kettle over low heat. Beat egg, baking soda, and salt into the sour cream in the bowl. Beat in 1 cup of the flour until well mixed. Continue to work in flour, $\frac{1}{4}$ cup at a time, until you have a dough that can be rolled. Roll the dough in a strip about 4 by 16 by $\frac{1}{4}$ inches. With a floured knife cut into 4-inch strips about $\frac{5}{8}$ inch wide.

Heat the lard to 375°F. Twist a strip like a corkscrew (it will stretch as you do); bring ends together and pinch them. Drop twisted dough in hot fat. In 2 minutes the dough should be brown on both sides, crisp and cooked through. If browning takes less time, the fat is too hot; if it takes more than 3 minutes, the fat is not hot enough.

Remove cooked doughnut to brown paper to drain and coat it with powdered sugar. Continue twisting and cooking the remaining dough strips. Serve the doughnuts immediately.

SWEDISH CRACKERS

These appeared on the Christmas menu in the Big Woods along with salt-rising bread, rye'n'injun bread, baked beans, vinegar pies, dried apple pies, cookies and molasses candy. According to Mrs. Roy Synstad of Nelson, Wisconsin, they are a traditional Scandinavian soft cracker prepared at Christmas time. Our recipe is adapted from one written out by Mrs. Synstad's mother early in this century and calling for "5¢ worth of baker's ammonia" and "5¢ worth of oil of lemon."

Baker's ammonia is a leavening agent still used in holiday

baking by cooks of Scandinavian and German heritage. It is ammonium carbonate, a salt sold in some pharmacies and in specialty food stores. Coarse salts should first be crushed (in a cloth with a mallet). All ammonia salts, coarse or fine, attract moisture and should be bought and kept in tight containers.

For about 36 Swedish crackers you will need:
Homogenized milk, $\frac{3}{4}$ cup
Ammonium carbonate, .35 ounce fine
Lard, $\frac{1}{2}$ cup, plus 2 teaspoons for pan greasing
Granulated sugar, $1\frac{1}{2}$ cups
Eggs, 2, beaten
Lemon extract, 2 teaspoons
Flour, 3 to 4 cups unbleached all-purpose

Saucepan, 1-pint; bowl, 1-pint; bowl, 2-quart; pastry surface
 and rolling pin; baking sheets, 2

In the saucepan scald $\frac{1}{2}$ cup milk. Put the ammonium carbonate in smaller bowl, pour the hot milk over it, and cover bowl with a plate or lid as the mixture foams up.

While the foamy mixture cools, grease the baking sheets. Blend lard and sugar in larger bowl. Beat into this the 2 eggs, lemon extract, remaining $\frac{1}{4}$ cup milk, and 2 cups of flour. Stir in the cooled milk mixture (no longer foamy) and another cup of flour to make a stiff batter. Add more flour, $\frac{1}{2}$ cup at a time, until the dough is firm enough to roll out.

On floured surface roll out the dough to a rectangle about 10 inches by 23 inches by $\frac{1}{4}$ inch. With a floured knife cut the dough into 2½-inch squares, about 36 in all. Preheat the oven to 350°F. Place squares on the baking sheets so they are not touching and prick them with a fork to make a design. Bake crackers in a moderate oven until they are lightly tanned, 10 to 15 minutes. Remove from pans to cool.

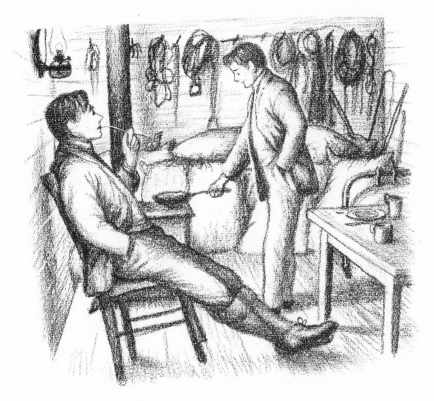

PANCAKE MEN

For breakfast there were pancakes, and Ma made a pancake man for each one of the children. Ma called each one in turn to bring her plate, and each could stand by the stove and watch, while with the spoonful of batter Ma put on the arms and the legs and the head. It was exciting to watch her turn the whole little man over, quickly and carefully, on a hot griddle. When it was done, she put it smoking hot on the plate.

LITTLE HOUSE IN THE BIG WOODS

To make pancake men you need a batter that flows well and a quick hand with the spoon. Ma's batter was neither a very rich one, like those made with heavy cream and eggs, nor a very frugal one, like those often stirred up out of stale bread crumbs and sour milk. In this recipe whole-wheat flour is mixed with white to resemble Ma's everyday flour, and cultured buttermilk is thinned a bit with water to resemble her buttermilk. Eat these pancake men with maple syrup.

For six pancake men (or 2 dozen 4-inch pancakes) you will need:
Baking soda, $\frac{1}{2}$ teaspoon
Whole-wheat flour, 1 cup
White flour, 1 cup unbleached all-purpose
Salt, $\frac{1}{2}$ teaspoon
Cultured buttermilk, 2 cups
1 egg, well beaten
Salt pork, $\frac{1}{4}$-pound chunk

Bowl or pitcher, 2-quart; griddle or skillet, 10-inch; spatula

Heat $\frac{1}{4}$ cup of water to a boil. Pour it on the baking soda (in a cup) to dissolve and cool while you proceed.

In pitcher or bowl mix two flours and salt. Stir in buttermilk and egg and beat well.

Heat the griddle until a few drops of water dance on it. Rub it well with fat salt pork. Stir cooled baking soda solution into batter with a few quick strokes.

Make pancake men one at a time in the center of the griddle. Fill a serving spoon with batter and pour it in adjoining circles to form torso, head, arms, and legs. When bubbles form and burst in batter turn man with spatula and cook equally long on the other side. Remove to warm plate. Grease the griddle again before the next pouring.

If you are preparing stacked round pancakes put a small piece of butter on each cake as you remove it to a warm platter. Use the first cake made for a top cover.

BUCKWHEAT PANCAKES

Then [Pa sat] down, as they urged him, and lifting the blanket cake on the untouched pile, he slipped from under it a section of the stack of hot, syrupy pancakes. Royal forked a brown slice of ham from the frying pan onto Pa's plate and Almanzo filled his coffee cup.

"You boys certainly live in the lap of luxury," Pa remarked. The pancakes were no ordinary buckwheat pancakes. Almanzo followed his mother's pancake rule and the cakes were light as foam, soaked through with melted brown sugar.

THE LONG WINTER

Just what was Mother Wilder's pancake rule? We guess that it was to start with an overnight sponge, as in breadmaking, for without that the cakes would scarcely be "light as foam." In Malone Mother Wilder made a sponge with fresh yeast, no doubt, and had plenty of butter to spread on the cakes as she stacked them. On the frontier Almanzo must have saved some of each batter as sponge for the next; molasses and melted brown sugar were his flavorings. From this yeast recipe you can reserve your own sponge for future pancake batches.

Another good rule is to use some whole-wheat flour, especially if you are not accustomed to the strong earthy flavor of buckwheat.

For 2 dozen 3-inch pancakes plus 1 cup of sponge you will need:
Molasses, 2 tablespoons
Yeast, 1 ounce or 2 small packages
Buckwheat flour, 2 cups
Whole-wheat flour, 1 cup
Baking soda, $\frac{1}{2}$ teaspoon
Salt, $\frac{1}{2}$ teaspoon
Drippings, 1 tablespoon
Salt pork, $\frac{1}{4}$-pound chunk
Brown sugar, $\frac{1}{2}$ cup

Bowl or pitcher, 2-quart; griddle or skillet, 10-inch; jar, 1-pint,
    with lid

The night (or 8 hours) before serving put $\frac{1}{2}$ cup of blood-warm water in the bowl or pitcher, stir in molasses, and crumble yeast on top. When yeast has softened, stir in another 2 cups of tap water and both the flours. Cover with a cloth and let stand at room temperature (under 70°F; refrigerate if room is hotter) to make the sponge.

Next morning remove 1 cup of the sponge to a jar as a starter for the next batch. Store in refrigerator. Dissolve baking soda and salt in $\frac{1}{2}$ cup of hot water and add drippings. Beat this into the sponge until well mixed.

Heat griddle until it makes water drops dance; grease it with salt pork. Pour one large test cake to start; use this to cover remaining cakes. Pour each cake 3 inches to 4 inches wide. Cook until bubbles form and burst, then turn and cook equally long on other side. As you stack finished cakes on a warm plate, sprinkle each with a little brown sugar.

The starter will keep for a number of days in the refrigerator. For your next batch of cakes, make the sponge by mixing starter with 2 tablespoons molasses, 2 cups bloodwarm water, $1\frac{1}{2}$ cups buckwheat flour, and 1 cup whole-wheat flour. Let stand overnight, then proceed as before, setting aside a new cup before adding final ingredients.

HULLED CORN

For supper, now, they often had hulled corn and milk. That was good, too. It was so good that Laura could hardly wait for the corn to be ready, after Ma started to hull it. It took two or three days to make hulled corn.

LITTLE HOUSE IN THE BIG WOODS

Hulled corn is dried yellow corn freed of its outer skin and cooked until the kernels are puffed and soft. It is also called hominy, although that, strictly speaking, is white corn.

The description in *Big Woods* is a good guide for those who want to produce a quantity of hulled corn exactly as Ma did it. If all you want is a sample of this delicious food, however, you can make it in a day, and you need not use lye (which can burn the skin) as Ma did.

You may use some of your own dried sweet corn (page 108), but big field corn kernels work better. If you can't get dried field corn from a farmer or feed store, buy one of the decorative ears sold in the supermarket at Thanksgiving time (provided it hasn't been lacquered for display use only) and watch the colors change as you proceed.

"Sometimes," we are told, the Ingallses "had hulled corn for breakfast, with maple syrup, and sometimes Ma fried the soft kernels in pork drippings. But Laura liked them best with milk." You can serve hulled corn warm in bowls with a pitcher of milk, as Laura did, or chill corn overnight for breakfast. In the morning, brown kernels in a skillet with a tablespoon of drippings. Or heat in water until boiling, drain, and serve warm in bowls with a pitcher of maple syrup.

For 3½ to 4 cups of hulled corn (hominy) you will need:
Field corn, one 11-inch ear or 1 cup kernels
Baking soda, 1 tablespoon

Kettle or saucepan, 6-cup; colander

Shell and wash the kernels and put them in kettle or saucepan to boil with 2 cups of water and the baking soda. Skim off anything that floats.

Reduce heat, cover, and simmer for about 3 hours, checking occasionally to see if more water is needed to prevent scorching.

When skins rub easily off a few kernels, drain off liquid and cover kernels with fresh water. Gathering up a small handful at a time, rub them well in your hands until the skins shred and the "eyes" loosen from the base of the kernels. Discard skins and eyes. With several pairs of hands the corn can quickly be rubbed and picked clean. Gather rubbed corn in colander and rinse well.

Return corn to pan, cover with water, and simmer. Check after 15 minutes: if water has become cloudy, change it. Continue simmering and changing water until water is clear and hominy is tender, about 2 to 3 hours. Drain.

HARDTACK

There was a great deal of work to be done, for Pa must leave early next morning. He set the old wagon bows on the wagon and pulled the canvas cover over them; it was almost worn out but it would do for the short trip. Aunt Docia and Carrie helped him pack the wagon, while Laura washed and ironed, and baked hardtack for the journey.

BY THE SHORES OF SILVER LAKE

Hardtack is the simplest of all nonperishable meals. Until as recently as World War I it was the staple food of traveling armies, who called it "sheet-iron," "tooth-dullers," "crown-breakers," and other names best forgotten. It was eaten dry only in emergencies, and then was more sucked on than chewed. Dipped in hot coffee, hardtack becomes edible; soaked well in water and fried in salt pork fat it is palatable as well.

All modern crackers are dimpled in the manner of hardtack, which was pricked with nail holes to keep it compact and breakable.

For 16 pieces of hardtack you will need:
White flour, 3+ cups unbleached all-purpose
Salt, 3 teaspoons

Bowl, 2-quart; rolling pin and breadboard; eight-penny nail;
    baking sheets, 2

Preheat the oven to 375°F. In the bowl mix 3 cups of flour with the salt. Add 1 cup of tap water and stir until it becomes too difficult. Knead dough in bowl with hand, adding more flour to make it very dry.

Press, pull, and roll the dough into a rectangle that can be divided into 3-inch squares of $\frac{1}{2}$-inch thickness. Use a table knife to cut dough into squares. Holding each square in hand, punch 16 holes through it with the nail, being careful not to hurt yourself. Place dough squares on ungreased baking sheets and bake for 30 minutes, until crisp and lightly browned. Cool before storing in a closed container.

Chapter
6

Foods from Gardens and Orchards

FRESH VEGETABLES FOR DINNER. To us they seem a commonplace, but to Laura they were something special and wonderful. Born before the time when lettuce heads could be grown in California and shipped to supermarkets in Maine, when even string beans in cans were a novelty, Laura could look forward to fresh plants for a meal only when her family had a garden. In that respect her life started with enough promise: the garden behind the Little House in the Big Woods provided carrots, cabbages, potatoes, turnips, pumpkins, squash, and probably more. But once the Ingallses left that garden behind, it was a long time before they enjoyed such bounty again. How disappointing it was, after almost a year of cornmeal and prairie hen and jack rabbit in Kansas, to leave behind their new prairie garden and the "little crumpled leaves of peas," the "tiny spears of onions," and the "little yellow bean-stem, coiled like a spring." How frustrating, in Plum Creek, to turn the soil and plant another garden, only to lose it to grasshoppers. Even on the claim, where their gardening efforts finally bore results, blackbirds and early frost took their toll.

Today more and more Americans are going "back to the soil," growing their own produce in backyard gardens. But they are scarcely reliving history. The plants they grow and the ways they prepare them for the table are mostly inventions of the last hundred years. In just a century—a very short time on Nature's calendar— even the soil itself has changed.

There is not a vegetable grown by the Ingallses that hasn't been changed in the years since by scientific breeding and hybridizing. America's most popular baking potato, the Idaho, was introduced to the world in the 1870's by the famed plant breeder Luther Burbank. Golden Bantam corn, a home garden favorite, was first offered for sale just after the turn of the century by W. Atlee Burpee, a seed salesman active in promoting new varieties. More than ninety per cent of American field corn acreage today is planted to hybrid corn unknown in 1920.

Some feel that plant foods are less flavorful as a result of scientific alterations. But just as surely as some have lost flavor, others have gained. Most vegetable plants are more productive, yielding more food per plant or per acre. Many are more resistant to common diseases and pests.

Garden soil has been altered by clearing, erosion, grazing, septic systems, single-crop farming, and pesticides. Chemical fertilizers, invented just before Laura's birth, and animal wastes have enriched the prairie soil first turned by the Ingallses.

Just as vegetables have changed, so have our ways of preparing them for the table. "Freshness" has always been prized by the cook and the diner, but even that notion alters with time. Today we know about vitamins and do our best not to wash or cook them away. Our forebears, knowing less about nutrition and more about other problems, were cautious. Soaking fresh-picked vegetables in spring water and thorough cooking were prescribed ways to cook them and to treat possible poisons, pests, and residue from animal waste.

Of all the changes in home food gardening since Laura's youth, perhaps the greatest has been in ways of preserving the harvest, for these in turn influence the choice of plantings. The Ingallses' gardens were heavily planted with root vegetables that could be stored where they grew or in the cellar; with thick-skinned squashes; and with food that could be dried, like corn and peas.

Surplus cucumbers, tomatoes, and beets could be pickled. Today the ease of home freezing encourages a greater emphasis on highly seasonal and perishable delicacies like asparagus and strawberries.

Between the centuries dominated by dry cold storage and pickling and the modern fast-freeze era came the heyday of home canning. New techniques perfected in 1803 for Napoleon's army were soon applied in commercial canneries, but not until after the Civil War were they made available to the housewife. Canning came into the home with the production of patent jars with lids that could be given an airtight seal. At first they held pickles and other old-fashioned preserves, but in time all manner of fresh vegetables and fruit were being put up. Home canning reached its zenith with the coming of the kitchen pressure canner; then it eventually yielded popularity to home freezing. Now a new era in food preservation may be upon us as we reexamine all these methods in terms of energy use.

The garden fruit best known to the Ingallses and Wilders was the apple. Only the orange has surpassed it as America's leading cultivated fruit. Seeds brought here from England by the colonists found favorable climate and soil and, eventually, a self-appointed distributor. The legendary Johnny Appleseed was a real man, John Chapman, who traveled through the Midwest at the start of the nineteenth century distributing and planting apple seeds with missionary zeal. By 1870 chance and the age-old practice of grafting (transferring twigs from one kind of tree to another) had produced more than a thousand native American varieties.

Most of these are now lost to us, as commercial growers concentrate on the dozen varieties that are most resistant to pests and cold and are best suited to mass cultivation, cold storage, and long-distance shipment. Undoubtedly the new mechanical apple picker will lead to still further selection.

Of the apples widely available today, Jonathan and Rome Beauty may have been known to the Wilders and Ingallses. The McIntosh had not yet spread from Canada through northern New York, replacing the Duchess apple that dominated Malone orchards in Almanzo's youth. Delicious and Golden Delicious were unheard of until this century.

MASHED POTATOES; POTATO CAKES

Almanzo's birthday, Christmas dinner in Malone, Thanksgiving dinner at Plum Creek, New England Supper at the church in DeSmet—whenever special occasions demanded special dinners, mashed potatoes were there.

You can best appreciate just how special mashed potatoes are when you make them without the aid of electrical appliances. Like ice cream and stiff egg whites, they require strenuous effort in the kitchen. The job goes easier with a "beetle" (masher) and a heavy whisk.

"Old" potatoes are best for mashing. Unlike "new" potatoes, which are dug when young and contain more water, old ones matured in the ground become mealy when boiled.

Potato cakes like those served at Ben Woodworth's birthday party are made with cold mashed potatoes. If you want enough for both mashed potatoes and cakes, double this recipe.

For six servings of mashed potatoes or 1 dozen potato cakes you will need:
"Old" potatoes, 6 medium
Salt
Homogenized milk, 1 cup
Butter "the size of an egg"
Pepper
Drippings, 2 tablespoons (for frying cakes)

Paring knife or peeler; kettle, 4-quart; saucepan, 1-pint; potato beetle; slotted spoon; heatproof serving dish (for mashed potatoes); skillet, 12-inch (for frying cakes)

FOR MASHED POTATOES

Scrub potatoes, and put them in kettle. Add 1 teaspoon of salt, cover with water, and simmer. After 15 minutes begin testing with fork; when potatoes are soft and flaky remove from heat, drain, and peel.

Heat milk in saucepan just to boiling point; add butter. Break up the potatoes in the kettle with the beetle and add half the buttery milk. With the beetle blend potatoes and liquid; then switch to slotted spoon and beat "as you would a cake"—that is, working always in the same direction to incorporate as much air as possible. Add more milk as needed until potatoes are creamy and quite wet.

Spoon potatoes carefully into the serving dish, sprinkle with salt and pepper, and place in warm oven until ready to serve. Browning on top, under the broiler if necessary, will give the dish a distinctive old-fashioned touch.

FOR POTATO CAKES

Divide day-old chilled mashed potatoes into number of servings desired. Heat drippings in skillet. Shape potatoes as you would hamburgers and fry them in hot fat, turning once after they have browned on the first side. Remove them to a warm platter as soon as they are crusty.

FRIED POTATOES

Slices of salt pork were frying, and Mrs. Brewster was slicing cold boiled potatoes into another frying pan on the stove. Johnny fussed in the bedroom, and Laura quickly pinned her braids, tied on her apron, and said, "Let me fix the potatoes while you dress him."

So while Mrs. Brewster brought Johnny to the stove and made him ready for breakfast, Laura finished slicing the potatoes, and salted and peppered and covered them. Then she turned the slices of meat and set the table neatly.

THESE HAPPY GOLDEN YEARS

Warm, filling, cheap, and quick to prepare, fried potatoes have long been a breakfast staple among working people. The Ingallses had them frequently for supper as well—served with a good deal more cheer than at the Brewsters'.

Usually potatoes are boiled before being fried, but they can also be "raw-fried," as Ma did them for the Boasts' surprise Christmas visit at Silver Lake. In that case the potatoes must first be peeled and sliced thin as possible and more time allowed for cooking under cover.

For six servings you will need:
Potatoes, 10 medium
Salt
Drippings (salt pork or bacon), 3 tablespoons
Pepper

Saucepan, 2-quart; skillet, 12-inch, with cover; paring knife

The night before serving, scrub potatoes and put them in saucepan with 1 teaspoon of salt. Cover with water. Simmer until potatoes can be stabbed with a fork but "still have a bone." Remove from heat and drain.

Peel immediately by holding hot potato on fork with one hand and stripping off brown skin with paring knife in the other. Return potatoes to saucepan, cover, and store in cool place overnight.

In the morning heat the drippings in the skillet. Cut the potatoes crosswise in $\frac{1}{8}$-inch slices. Put slices in skillet, season with salt and pepper, and stir. Cover and cook through, about 8 minutes. Remove the lid, stir again and finish browning, and serve up on plates.

HASHED BROWN POTATOES

Outdoors was crisp and cold. Sunshine gilded the frosty windows, and in the house everyone was hearty and cheerful. How the travelers did enjoy that breakfast! They praised everything they ate. The biscuits were light and flaky, the fried potatoes were brown and finely hashed, the slices of fat pork were thin and crisp, and the gravy was smooth and brown and creamy. There was hot brown-sugar syrup, and plenty of fragrant steaming tea.

BY THE SHORES OF SILVER LAKE

Company like Reverend Alden would have warranted hashed brown potatoes instead of the more ordinary fried. Even today, "hash-browns," like the eggs they usually accompany, can be something quite out of the ordinary. The reputation of many a roadside restaurant in America is built on the quality of its breakfast hash-browns.

Good hashed browns are finely chopped but held together by a crunchy brown crust. Do try them with Fried Salt Pork with Gravy (page 18) when it is crisp and cold outdoors!

For six servings you will need:
Potatoes, 10 medium
Drippings (salt pork or bacon)
Salt and pepper

Saucepan, 2-quart; chopper and bowl; skillet, 12-inch, with
    cover

Starting the night before serving, proceed as for Fried Potatoes (previous recipe) with this change: instead of slicing the potatoes quite so thin, cut them $\frac{1}{4}$ inch thick. Place slices a handful at a time in the chopping bowl and chop to cubes. Put cubes in hot skillet with drippings, season with salt and pepper. Cook through, about 8 minutes, turning halfway through. When nicely browned, serve up on plates.

CREAMED CARROTS

Almanzo ate four large helpings of apples 'n' onions fried together. He ate roast beef and brown gravy, and mashed potatoes and creamed carrots and boiled turnips, and countless slices of buttered bread with crab-apple jelly.

FARMER BOY

Hoeing and helping to harvest two hundred bushels didn't seem to diminish Almanzo's appetite for carrots. At the table he ate them creamed and candied, and probably mashed and stewed. In the barnyard, while breaking the calves Star and Bright to the yoke, he ate raw carrots meant only for animals. Laura Wilder must have liked raw carrots, too; she wrote, "The outside part is best. It comes off in a thick, solid ring, and it is sweet. The inside part is juicier, and clear like yellow ice, but it has a thin, sharp taste."

For six servings you will need:
Carrots, 3 pounds, without tops
Chicken or veal broth (or water), 1 cup
Butter, 2 tablespoons, soft
Flour, 2 tablespoons
Heavy or sour cream, $\frac{1}{4}$ cup
Salt and freshly ground pepper

Saucepan, 2-quart; small bowl

Scrub carrots with a stiff brush and slice them into the saucepan, cutting disks about $\frac{1}{8}$ inch thick. Add broth (or water), cover, and simmer until a fork will puncture a slice (about 15 minutes).

Meanwhile in a small bowl blend butter and flour with a fork. Gradually work in cream to make a thin paste.

When carrots are tender remove pan from heat and stir in paste: blend well with a wooden spoon, but be careful not to bruise the carrots. Return to heat just until the cream bubbles.

Turn into a serving dish and sprinkle with salt and pepper.

DRIED CORN; CREAMED CORN

After dinner, Pa brought another armful of blackbirds and an armful of corn.

"We might as well figure that the crop's gone," he said. "This corn's a little too green, but we'd better eat what we can of it before the blackbirds get it all."

"I don't know why I didn't think of it sooner!" Ma exclaimed. "Laura and Carrie, hurry and pick every ear that's possibly old enough to make dried corn. Surely we can save a little, to eat next winter. . . . we'll boil this corn, and cut it off the cobs, to dry."

LITTLE TOWN ON THE PRAIRIE

When he saw the dried corn later Pa remarked, "That's an Indian idea." In fact, the Indians dried the whole ear, the way farmers still dry feed corn.

A recipe is included here for dried corn as it was served at the New England Supper—"soaked soft again and cooked with cream." Dried corn may also be used for parching (page 212) and for succotash (page 111).

For 3 heaping cups of dried corn you will need:
Green field corn or ripe sweet corn, six 9-inch ears

Kettle, 2-gallon; sharp knife; an old tablecloth or equivalent; cheesecloth, curtain, or other loosely woven cloth

FOR CREAMED CORN:
Dried Corn, $1\frac{1}{2}$ cups
Cream, 2 tablespoons heavy, or 2 tablespoons homogenized milk and 1 teaspoon butter
Salt
Pepper

Saucepan, 1-quart

Half-fill the kettle with water and bring it to a lively boil. Strip the ears of husks and silk; cut off cob ends flat. To "set" the juices drop the ears into the boiling water and leave them until the boiling resumes, about 3 minutes. Remove ears to cloth to drain.

Now follow the rest of Mrs. Wilder's account, below. Cutting goes best if you stand each ear on the flattened end and cut straight down with a sawing motion. Corn can also be dried on baking sheets in a 150°F oven overnight and through the following day. For outdoor drying in humid climates check directions for Sun-Dried Wild Fruit (page 53).

"There is a knack to cutting corn from a cob. The knife must slice evenly, the whole length of the rows, cutting deep enough to get almost the whole kernel, but not so deep as to cut even an edge from the sharp pocket in which each kernel grows. The kernels fall away in milky slabs, moist and sticky.

"Ma spread these on a clean, old tablecloth laid outdoors in the sunshine, and she covered them with another cloth, to keep away the blackbirds and the chickens and the flies. The hot sun would dry the corn, and next winter, soaked and boiled, it would be good eating."

Boiling, *then* soaking, makes just as good eating and goes faster. For six servings of creamed corn, wash $1\frac{1}{2}$ cups dried corn, put in a 1-quart saucepan, and cover with water. Bring to a boil; remove from heat; cover with lid. Set aside until corn has absorbed the water, about 1 hour.

Just before mealtime reheat the corn. Stir in 2 tablespoons of heavy cream or 2 tablespoons of milk and 1 teaspoon of butter. Salt and pepper to taste. If the corn is green field corn a teaspoon of sugar may be needed. Serve piping hot.

FRIED PARSNIPS

Here is a vegetable popular a century ago that may be unknown to some "Little House" readers. A long ivory-colored root, the plump parsnip has the durable qualities of the turnip but a flavor more delicate, almost nutty. It appeared on the Wilders' Christmas table as "pale fried parsnips."

Today the market offers parsnips as small and thin-skinned as carrots, equally good raw or sliced in rounds and lightly cooked. To fry parsnips as Mrs. Wilder did, however, you will need the big old-fashioned variety. Notice that for frying the long roots are sliced *lengthwise*.

For six servings you will need:
Large parsnips, 3 pounds, without tops
Flour, $\frac{1}{2}$ cup
Salt and pepper, a pinch each
Butter, 4 to 6 tablespoons
Vinegar

Kettle, 4-quart; skillet, 12-inch

Wash parsnips and trim off tails. Simmer in the kettle in water to cover for about 15 minutes, until a fork will just penetrate. Drain, scrape off skins with a table knife, and chill parsnips.

Slice the cool parsnips lengthwise in strips $\frac{1}{8}$ inch thick. Season flour with salt and pepper, and dredge each strip in it. Heat 2 tablespoons of butter in skillet until foamy, then add as many slices as will cover the pan bottom. Brown lightly for a few minutes; turn and cook through, about 10 minutes in all. Remove to warm platter. Repeat until all slices are cooked, adding butter to the skillet as needed.

At table these are best eaten with a sprinkling of vinegar.

SUCCOTASH

No county fair dinner was complete without succotash, and no American cookbook is complete without a recipe for this native dish that combines two vegetables just as the Indians grew them. The Indians introduced white settlers to corn and showed them that planting in rows was more efficient than scattering seed broadside. That way the cornstalks could serve as poles for the beans planted between the rows.

By the time the Franklin County Fair opened on a frosty October morning the season for fresh succotash was past. What Almanzo and his family ate was made from canned or dried vegetables. The beans would have been shell beans, ordinary pole beans grown to maturity, shelled, and dried. Where these are not available the now-universal lima bean can be substituted.

For six servings you will need:
Dried shell or lima beans, 1 cup
Dried Corn (page 108), 1 cup
Butter, 1 tablespoon
Cream, $\frac{1}{4}$ cup
Salt and pepper

Bowls, 1-quart, 2; saucepan, 2-quart

Three hours before mealtime put dried beans and corn in separate bowls, wash, and drain. Fill the bowls with boiling water, stir the vegetables, and cover them with plates. Let stand until water is absorbed, about 2 hours.

If beans are still not tender, transfer them to saucepan and simmer about 20 minutes, adding water if needed to prevent burning. Add corn and quickly cook away any remaining liquid. Add butter and coat vegetables well; add cream and cook until it is hot. Salt and pepper to taste and transfer to a warm serving dish.

LETTUCE LEAVES WITH VINEGAR AND SUGAR

The day was ending in perfect satisfaction. They were all there together. All the work, except the supper dishes, was done until tomorrow. They were all enjoying good bread and butter, fried potatoes, cottage cheese, and lettuce leaves sprinkled with vinegar and sugar.

LITTLE TOWN ON THE PRAIRIE

What kind of lettuce did Ma grow in DeSmet? An 1888 Bulletin from the nearby Dakota Agricultural College and Experiment Station (now South Dakota State University) tells us, "So many excellent varieties of this vegetable are now offered that it is hard to find an inferior sort." One certainty is that it was *not* iceberg, a modern lettuce bred with tight leaves and a firm head suited to interstate shipping. It was probably a loose-leaf variety, such as Simpson, but in this recipe you can also use butterhead (Bibb or Boston) or romaine (cos) lettuces—just so they're garden-fresh.

Some Americans still prefer sugar and vinegar to the oil and vinegar dressing introduced after the Civil War by enthusiasts of French salads. *The Pioneer Cookbook,* published by the Daughters of Utah Pioneers, gives this recipe for "Lettuce at Its Best": *Shredded lettuce; 1 cup onions chopped fine; $\frac{1}{2}$ cup home-made vinegar; $\frac{1}{4}$ cup water; tsp sugar; pepper and salt to taste.*

An even simpler recipe follows.

For six servings you will need:
Lettuce, 1 full head fresh garden variety
Vinegar in cruet
Sugar in bowl

Large serving bowl; kitchen towels, 2

Wash lettuce by dipping leaves quickly in a basin of cold water (a running spigot or pump wastes water; soaking leaves wastes vitamins). Drain on kitchen towels; pat dry. Arrange in bowl and take to the table with cruet and sugar bowl.

At the table take a leaf in your fingers, sprinkle it with some vinegar and sugar, roll it tight, and eat it as you would a celery stalk.

RIPE TOMATOES WITH SUGAR AND CREAM

A century before Laura was born tomatoes were thought by many Americans to be poisonous, perhaps because the green stems and leaves can be fatal to certain animals. Even in her youth many people would not eat tomatoes raw.

Not so the Ingalls family. When they finally had a successful garden on the Dakota claim they enjoyed tomatoes at their very best —fresh from the vine.

The tomatoes were probably quite tart and needed sugar. We know that turn-of-the-century plant scientists worked to improve sweetness, hardiness, disease resistance, and yield. Continuous selective breeding has produced some excellent home- and truck-garden varieties.

Greenhouse cultivation and gas ripening have made tomatoes available the year around. But fresh-picked, sun-ripened tomatoes are a summer specialty whose flavor simply can't be matched.

For six servings you will need:
Red-ripe tomatoes, garden-fresh, 4 pounds
Parsley, lettuce, or wild sorrel, a few leaves
Medium cream, 1 cup
Sugar in bowl

Kettle of boiling water or a candle

Pick the tomatoes in the morning, before the dew is gone, taking only those that lift easily from their stems. Wipe dry and set in a cool (not cold) place until mealtime.

To peel the skin easily, insert a fork in the tomato's stem end and plunge the tomato for 3 seconds in boiling water. Or rotate it next to an open candle flame until the entire surface has been seared. Without removing the fork peel off the skin with a knife. Cut the tomatoes crosswise in slices about $\frac{3}{8}$ inch thick and arrange on a platter with some greens—parsley, lettuce, or sorrel. At the table, each person adds cream and sugar to taste.

BAKED HUBBARD SQUASH

At other times they had baked Hubbard squash for dinner. The rind was so hard that Ma had to take Pa's ax to cut the squash into pieces. When the pieces were baked in the oven, Laura loved to spread the soft insides with butter and then scoop the yellow flesh from the rind and eat it.

LITTLE HOUSE IN THE BIG WOODS

Some squashes are called winter squashes because they mature in the fall with thick skins that protect them for winter storage. Probably the toughest skin of all belonged to the Hubbard, a very large, warty, dark-green, football-shaped squash that was a good "keeper" in the days before refrigeration.

In our century the hard-to-cut skin has become a liability, and growers have responded to a preference for smaller squashes that are easier to cut. If you find a Hubbard in the store at all, it is likely to be a baby variety or a large one cut into pieces.

Perhaps you don't care for thin-skinned summer squashes (zucchini, yellow squash, etc.). Don't let that keep you from trying Hubbard squash as Laura ate it. With a little brown sugar added it is almost a confection.

For six servings you will need:
Hubbard squash, 3 babies or 2 pounds cut in serving pieces
Butter, 6 teaspoons
Salt and pepper

Dripping pans, 2

Halve the baby squashes and remove the seeds. Large squashes bought in pieces are usually free of seeds.

Rub the fleshy surfaces well with butter to prevent drying in the oven. Place pieces skin side down in dripping pans. Add boiling water to pans to a depth of about $\frac{1}{2}$ inch.

Place pans in preheated 350°F oven and bake until a fork will easily penetrate the yellow flesh, about $1\frac{1}{2}$ to 2 hours.

Serve each piece with a pinch of butter and a shake of salt and pepper on top. Or scoop the yellow flesh from the rind into a warm serving bowl.

RAW TURNIP SNACKS

. . . it was good to know that there were turnips enough in the cellar to last all winter long. There would be boiled turnips, and mashed turnips and creamed turnips. And in the winter evenings a plate of raw turnips would be on the table by the lamp; they would peel off the thick rinds and eat the raw turnips in crisp, juicy slices.

ON THE BANKS OF PLUM CREEK

The Ingallses' experience shows why turnips were a popular farm crop. As root foods in the soil they could survive grasshopper attacks and prairie fires. With their dense flesh and thick skins they could be held in storage through the winter. They were versatile as table food and fodder.

We urge those who are not moved by cooked turnips to try raw turnip slices as a snack, with or without salt. Make sure you have the true purple-topped kind and not "yellow turnips," which are really rutabagas.

Scrub each turnip you use, but peel only what you eat, as the Ingallses did, for peeled slices left in the air too long will discolor. Slicing takes a good sharp knife and a practiced hand.

Low-calorie turnips are excellent snacks for modern people whose problem is too many, rather than too few, good things to eat at hand.

MASHED TURNIPS

No farmers' feast of a century ago was complete without mashed turnips. Often, as at the Wilders' Christmas dinner and the DeSmet church's New England Supper, they sat side by side on the table with mashed potatoes and squash.

On Plum Creek Laura helped pull the ripe turnips from the ground and cut off the "juicy green tops" to feed Spot and the calf. Later in the winter the turnips themselves might be used for fodder. Nowadays turnips and their greens are often sold as two vegetables, and rutabagas are often labeled "yellow turnips."

For six servings you will need:
Turnips, $2\frac{1}{2}$ to 3 pounds, without tops
Butter, 3 tablespoons
Salt and pepper

Paring knife; kettle, 2-gallon; potato beetle or masher

Wash turnips and peel them with vertical strokes of a paring knife. Slice thin across grain to break vertical fibers. Place in kettle with a little water—$\frac{1}{4}$ to $\frac{1}{2}$ cup should do—and simmer, covered, until tender. This will take 20 to 30 minutes. Remove cover for last few minutes to cook away excess water.

Add butter and sprinklings of salt and pepper, and mash turnips. Return to burner to heat through, then remove to a warm serving dish.

STEWED PUMPKIN

Pumpkins were grown by the Indians before the first settlers arrived from Europe. They remained popular garden vegetables because they were easy to grow and store and could be served as either a vegetable or a sweet. An English cooking guide of 1842, noting that in America "the pumpkin is grown for show rather than use," makes us think of pumpkin-growing contests and Almanzo's successful entry at the county fair. The same guide points out that Americans stew, rather than slice, their pumpkin for pies.

Stewed pumpkin was served at the table like mashed potatoes, with salt, pepper, and butter—but only after the quantity needed for pies had first been claimed in the kitchen.

For a recipe, follow the description below from *Little House in the Big Woods.* Allow at least five hours' cooking time. If your large kettle has a lid you may cover it for the first two hours and save yourself stirring; after that, the accumulated liquid must cook away and you must stir it regularly.

For 1½ quarts (enough for a 9-inch pie and six dinner servings) you will need:

A ripe pumpkin, about 10 pounds
Salt and pepper to taste
Butter, 2 tablespoons

Cleaver or large knife; paring knife; kettle, 2-gallon

"With the butcher knife Ma cut the big, orange-colored pumpkins into halves. She cleaned the seeds out of the center and cut the pumpkin into long slices, from which she pared the rind. Laura helped her cut the slices into cubes.

"Ma put the cubes into the big iron pot on the stove, poured in some water, and then watched while the pumpkin slowly boiled down, all day long. All the water and the juice must be boiled away, and the pumpkin must never burn.

"The pumpkin was a thick, dark, good-smelling mass in the kettle. It did not boil like water, but bubbles came up in it and suddenly exploded, leaving holes that closed quickly. Every time a bubble exploded, the rich, hot, pumpkin smell came out.

"Laura stood on a chair and watched the pumpkin for Ma, and stirred it with a wooden paddle. She held the paddle in both hands and stirred carefully, because if the pumpkin burned there wouldn't be any pumpkin pies."

When the pumpkin has reached the texture of applesauce, turn up the heat for about 10 minutes more of cooking to dry it out, watching closely and stirring frequently. Remove from heat and take out 2 cups of pumpkin for a pie. Keep the rest warm until you can serve it seasoned with salt and pepper, dotted with butter, and accompanied with bread. Young children should be permitted to "make the rich, brown, stewed pumpkin into pretty shapes" before eating.

PUMPKIN PIE

Pumpkin pie was part of every special dinner in the "Little House" saga, whether for threshers, for a social or fair, or for a holiday celebration. Unlike English pies, made with slices of pumpkin and apples, American pumpkin pies have always used stewed pumpkin, made into a custard with milk and eggs. The traditional flavorings—cinnamon, nutmeg, ginger, and cloves—can be bought as "pumpkin pie spice." The richness depended on the cook's resources: a standard recipe (for an unspecified number of pies), passed on from colonial times, called for three pints of heavy cream and nine eggs!

The recipe here is for pumpkin pie as it may have been made in the Big Woods, with few eggs and with brown sugar and maple flavoring standing in for Ma's maple sugar.

For a 9-inch pie (six to eight servings) you will need:
Stewed Pumpkin, 2 cups (see previous recipe)
Common Family Paste for Pies (page 194)
Eggs, 2
Brown sugar, $\frac{2}{3}$ cup
Rich milk or half-and-half, $1\frac{1}{4}$ cups
Salt, a pinch
Maple flavoring, 1 teaspoon
Ground cinnamon, cloves, nutmeg, ginger—a pinch of whatever
    you have

Pie pan, 9-inch; bowl, 3-quart

Prepare Stewed Pumpkin according to recipe. Prepare Common Family Paste for Pies and line a buttered pie pan with it.

Preheat the oven to 425°F. In the bowl beat the eggs well, then beat in the brown sugar, milk, salt, maple flavoring, spices, and pumpkin. Pour this into the pie shell and place it on the center oven rack to bake at 425° for 10 minutes. Reduce the heat to 350° and continue to bake until the crust is brown and the pumpkin custard is firm (a knife inserted should come out clean and dry). This will take about 40 minutes in all. Cool but do not chill before serving.

GREEN PUMPKIN PIE

> *"Caroline, however did you manage to make a pie?" Pa exclaimed. "What kind of pie is it?"*
>
> *"Taste it and see!" said Ma. She cut a piece and put it on his plate.*
>
> *Pa cut off the point with his fork and put it in his mouth. "Apple pie! Where in the world did you get apples?"*
>
> *Carrie could keep still no longer. She almost shouted, "It's pumpkin! Ma made it of green pumpkin!"*
>
> *Pa took another small bite and tasted it carefully. "I'd never have guessed it," he said. "Ma always could beat the nation cooking."*
>
> THE LONG WINTER

Improvising a successful treat when the larder is low is a special pleasure for cooks and eaters alike. That was such a happy supper, the author recalls, Laura wanted it never to end.

To reproduce this surprise will take ingenuity in *finding* an unripe pumpkin if you don't have a garden. You will need adult cooperation, but be sure not to let everyone in on the secret.

If you have no homemade vinegar, substitute hard cider or frozen cider concentrate, both of which have more character than distilled commercial vinegar.

For a 9-inch covered pie (six to eight servings) you will need:
Common Family Paste for Pies, double recipe (page 194)
A green (unripe) pumpkin, about 4 pounds
Brown sugar, 1 cup
Ground nutmeg, cloves, cinnamon—small pinch of each or
        large pinch of one
Vinegar, $\frac{1}{3}$ cup homemade (page 131), or hard cider or 3
        tablespoons frozen cider concentrate
Butter, 1 teaspoon

Pastry surface and rolling pin; pie pan, 9-inch; paring knife;
        knife, 8-inch; bowl, 2-quart

Line the buttered pie pan with half the pie paste. Chill top crust. Preheat oven to 425°F.

With the large knife cut the pumpkin in quarters. Remove the seeds. With the paring knife scrape away the outer skin and cut the flesh into crosswise slices resembling apple slices. The bowl is for these slices.

Bearing in mind that her cup measure was smaller than yours (so use the quantities above), follow Ma, who "put the crust in the pie pan and covered the bottom with brown sugar and spices. Then she filled the crust with thin slices of the green pumpkin. She poured half a cup of vinegar over them, put a small piece of butter on top, and laid the top crust over all."

Crimp the edges of the pie and vent the top. Bake at 425° for 15 minutes, then reduce heat to 350° and bake 35 to 40 minutes longer, or until nicely browned.

APPLE TURNOVERS

> *At noontime everyone was allowed to move about the schoolroom and talk quietly. Eliza Jane opened the dinner-pail on her desk. It held bread-and-butter and sausage, doughnuts and apples, and four delicious apple-turnovers, their plump crusts filled with melting slices of apple and spicy brown juice.*
>
> *After Almanzo had eaten every crumb of his turnover and licked his fingers, he took a drink of water from the pail with a dipper in it, on a bench in the corner. Then he put on his cap and coat and mittens and went out to play.*
>
> FARMER BOY

Here is a school lunch guaranteed to attract company. The "plump crusts" were probably puff paste (see Fine Pie Paste, page 196); a butterworker of Mother Wilder's experience would have had no difficulty layering and rolling the paste and butter.

However, ordinary pie paste was just as frequently used for fruit turnovers, and that's what we recommend to those who have not yet developed the puff-paste knack. We also suggest that bulky apple slices be chopped into more "turnable" pieces, and we give directions for baking as well as pan frying.

For six large turnovers you will need:
Common Family Paste for Pies, double recipe (page 194)
Tart apples, 3 or 4 (about 1 pound)
Brown sugar, $\frac{2}{3}$ cup
Ground cinnamon or nutmeg, $\frac{1}{4}$ teaspoon
Butter, 2 teaspoons
Powdered sugar, 6 teaspoons

Chopper and bowl; bowl, 2-quart; pastry board and rolling pin; baking sheets, 2, or skillet, 12-inch

Following the recipe for Common Family Paste, double the quantities and prepare two balls of dough. Chill both while you prepare the filling.

Peel, core, slice, and chop apples. Mix them in the 2-quart bowl with brown sugar and spice. Set aside to chill.

Roll the first dough ball to a rectangle 5 by 15 by $\frac{1}{8}$ inches. Cut it into three 5-inch squares. Using a fork (so the juice stays in the bowl), place about 3 tablespoons of apples in the center of each square. Wet the edges of each square and fold over each pastry to enclose the apples in a triangular pocket. Seal edges by pressing with fork tines. Cook the first three while you use the remaining dough and apples to prepare the other turnovers. Any leftover apple pieces and liquid can go into your vinegar jug (page 132).

TO BAKE THE TURNOVERS

Preheat the oven to 425°F as you butter the baking sheets. Transfer turnovers to sheets and bake 20 to 25 minutes, until nicely browned.

TO FRY THE TURNOVERS

Melt half the butter in the skillet, add half the turnovers and cook on medium high heat 10 minutes to a side. Repeat with remaining pastries.

Dust warm turnovers with powdered sugar and let them cool before packing them in your lunch pail.

APPLE PIE

As soon as Mother finished straining the milk, they all sat down and Father asked the blessing for breakfast.

There was oatmeal with plenty of thick cream and maple sugar. There were fried potatoes, and the golden buckwheat cakes, as many as Almanzo wanted to eat, with sausages and gravy or with butter and maple syrup. There were preserves and jams and jellies and doughnuts. But best of all Almanzo liked the spicy apple pie, with its thick, rich juice and its crumbly crust. He ate two big wedges of the pie.

FARMER BOY

Thick, rich juice and crumbly crust were the marks of a well-made apple pie. Not-so-well-made ones had thick crusts made soggy with thin juice. Or the juice cooked over and gummed up the pie pan and oven.

How to prevent runovers has always been one of the challenges of baking fruit pies. Nowadays cornstarch is often used to thicken and hold juices. Before it was invented, cooks sometimes swathed their pie pans in wet cloths. Or, as in this recipe, they sometimes used flour, sprinkled carefully so it would not form pasty lumps.

For a 9-inch covered pie (six to eight servings) you will need:
Common Family Paste for Pie, double recipe (page 194)
Lemon, 1
Tart apples, about 2 pounds
Brown sugar, ¾ cup
Flour, 3 teaspoons
Ground cinnamon, cloves, nutmeg—pinch of one or all
Butter, 1 tablespoon
Heavy cream

Pie pan, 9-inch; bowl, 2-quart

For a breakfast pie, prepare a double recipe of Common Family Paste and line the buttered pie pan with half the paste. Chill top crust dough. Preheat the oven to 425°F.

Prepare zest (peel) and juice of lemon: With a sharp knife score the yellow peel in cross-hatch pattern and shave off, taking care to avoid white layer underneath. Set aside. Halve the lemon, press the flesh over the tines of a fork, and squeeze into the bowl (the fork will prevent squirting).

Peel, core, and slice the apples into the bowl with juice. An easy way to do this with only a knife is to quarter the apples, then peel the quarters, cut out the cores, and slice. Toss the slices with the juice.

Line the bottom piecrust with a layer of apple slices. Strew the layer with a third of the brown sugar and a third of the flour. Repeat layers until these ingredients are used up. Strew the zest and spices over the top and dot with butter. Cover with top crust, crimp the edges, and prick with a fork to vent.

Bake in a 425° oven for 10 minutes, then reduce heat to 350° and bake 30 to 35 minutes more, until crust is brown. Serve warm in bowls with a pitcher of heavy cream.

BIRDS'-NEST PUDDING

"It takes a great deal to feed a growing boy," Mother said. And she put a thick slice of birds'-nest pudding on his bare plate, and handed him the pitcher of sweetened cream speckled with nutmeg.

Almanzo poured the heavy cream over the apples nested in the fluffy crust. The syrupy brown juice curled up around the edges of the cream. Almanzo took up his spoon and ate every bit.

FARMER BOY

The author's mouth-watering description suggests she would have approved the dish for growing girls as well.

Birds'-nest pudding was to Mother Wilder's generation what apple brown betty is to ours—a standard apple dessert with many individual variations. Whole peeled and cored apples were basic; the "nest" in which they were baked might be a custard, biscuit dough, or pie pastry. This New England version once used maple sugar and has a truly fluffy crust that is handsome as it is delicious.

For six servings you will need:
Butter, $\frac{1}{2}$ teaspoon
Tart apples, 6 (about 2 pounds)
Brown sugar, 1 cup
Ground nutmeg, $\frac{1}{2}$ teaspoon
Eggs, 3
Homogenized milk, 1 cup
Maple flavoring, 1 teaspoon
Flour, 1 cup
Cream of tartar, 1 teaspoon
Baking powder, $\frac{1}{2}$ teaspoon
Salt, $\frac{1}{2}$ teaspoon
Powdered sugar, $\frac{1}{2}$ cup
Heavy cream, 1 pint

Baking dish, 2-quart; apple corer and paring knife; bowl, 2-quart; platter, 12-inch; bowl, 1-quart;

Butter the baking dish. Peel and core the apples and place them in the dish. Fill the holes with brown sugar, pressing slightly, and sprinkle half the nutmeg on top. Place in preheated 350°F oven to start baking while you prepare the batter.

Separate the eggs, putting yolks in the larger bowl and whites on the platter. Beat whites with a fork or whisk until they no longer slip from the tilted platter. Beat the yolks until they change color; stir in milk and maple flavoring. In smaller bowl mix flour, cream of tartar, baking powder, salt, and any remaining brown sugar. Stir this mixture quickly into the liquid. Fold the egg whites into this thin batter.

Pour the batter evenly over and around the partly cooked apples and return dish to the oven, baking it until the crust has browned, another 45 minutes to 1 hour.

While the pudding bakes, stir the powdered sugar and remaining nutmeg into a pitcher of heavy cream. Take the finished pudding directly to the table before it "falls," and turn each serving onto a plate so the apple is "nested in the fluffy crust." Pass the pitcher of sweetened cream.

FRIED APPLES'N'ONIONS

He knelt on the ice, pushing sawdust into the cracks with his mittened hands, and pounding it down with a stick as fast as he could, and he asked Royal,

"What would you like best to eat?"

They talked about spareribs, and turkey with dressing, and baked beans, and crackling cornbread, and other good things. But Almanzo said that what he liked most in the world was fried apples'n'onions.

When, at last, they went in to dinner, there on the table was a big dish of them! Mother knew what he liked best, and she had cooked it for him.

FARMER BOY

This is a "country" dish, seldom mentioned in cookbooks but recalled by many oldtimers. Some feel the sugar essential; others call it "a sin." If you share Almanzo's enthusiasm you might also like to try fried apples'n'onions with fried potatoes (page 104) for breakfast sometime.

For six servings you will need:
Bacon or salt pork, $\frac{1}{2}$ pound, sliced
Yellow onions, 6 (2 pounds)
Tart apples, 6 (2 pounds)
Brown sugar, 2 tablespoons

Skillet, 12-inch, with cover; apple corer

Fry bacon or salt pork slices in the skillet until brown and crisp. Set them aside on a warm serving platter.

While the meat is frying, peel the onions, leaving the stems to hold for slicing. To prevent eyes from watering hold a slice of bread in your teeth while you slice onions as thin as possible. Discard stems.

Core the apples and cut them crosswise in circles about $\frac{1}{4}$ inch thick. Apple skins help the slices keep their shape and add color to the dish, so don't peel unless skins are tough or scarred.

Drain all but 1 tablespoon of fat from the skillet, then add the onion slices. Cook them over medium-high heat for about 3 minutes. Cover with apple slices in an even layer. Sprinkle brown sugar over all, cover the skillet, and cook until tender, a few minutes more. Stir only to prevent scorching. Remove to the warm plate with bacon or salt pork slices.

DRIED APPLES

The oats were ripe, standing thick and tall and yellow. The wheat was golden, darker than the oats. The beans were ripe, and pumpkins and carrots and turnips and potatoes were ready to gather.

There was no rest and no play for anyone now. They all worked from
candle-light to candle-light. Mother and the girls were making cucum-
ber pickles . . . they were drying corn and apples, and making preserves.
FARMER BOY

Sun drying is a fine way to preserve small fruits that ripen in summer, but by the time apple-harvest season arrives in upstate New York, there are too few sunny days for such activity. The Wilder women dried their apples indoors by the cookstoves, using one or both of two time-honored techniques.

Start with tart, firm apples like pippin or McIntosh. Use freshly picked apples only; those held in cold storage for out-of-season sale become unattractively dark when dried. Commercially grown apples are heavily sprayed and should be washed and wiped. Peel them only if the skins are tough.

The quick way using the least skill is to slice the apples crosswise in $\frac{1}{8}$-inch disks and slip them onto string or rods. Hang the string or prop the rods in a warm dry place like a furnace room or sun porch. Curtain rods over a sunny window may be used, or a laundry rack near a radiator. Leave hanging until the apples are leathery and can be squeezed without juicing.

For more compact storage and more versatile use, apples can be dried in smaller slices. Quarter the apples, core them, and slice them $\frac{1}{8}$ inch thick. Spread them on cloth-covered trays and place them in a cooling oven overnight, as in the directions for Dried Corn, page 108. The oven Mother Wilder used for baking beans overnight was probably excellent for apple drying. When the slices are leathery, store them in sterilized dry jars (or plastic bags) with as little air space as possible.

To prepare applesauce, stew the slices according to the recipe for Stewed Dried Fruit (page 54). Allow about $1\frac{1}{2}$ dozen rings or 1 cup of slices per person. Beat the stewed fruit into a sauce or press it through a colander before serving. Sauce made from apple rings must be strained to separate out cores and skins. To use dried apples in pie, see the following recipe.

DRIED APPLE AND RAISIN PIE

> *. . . Ma set the sponge for light bread that night, and she put the dried apples to soak for pies.*
> *Laura did not need to be called next morning. She . . . and Carrie carefully picked dried raisins from their long stems and carefully took the seeds out of each one. Ma stewed the dried apples, mixed the raisins with them, and made pies.*

THE LONG WINTER

For this recipe you will be spared Laura and Carrie's chore, for the raisins you buy will be free of stems and seeds. They will come from California, which succeeded Spain as the raisin capital of the world with the introduction of Thompson seedless white grapes. If you have a choice, buy dark raisins. They are sun-dried grapes, as Ma's would have been. Golden grapes are, oddly enough, sulfured and oven-dried to retain their natural color!

This pie bears a resemblance to mince pie—close enough to intrigue mincemeat fanciers, different enough to attract mincemeat avoiders. If you forget to soak the apples overnight, a half hour in freshly boiled water will soften the slices just as well.

For a 9-inch covered pie (six to eight servings) you will need:
Dried apple slices, 3 cups (see previous recipe)
Common Family Paste for Pies, double recipe (page 194)
Seedless dark raisins, 1 cup
White flour, 1 tablespoon unbleached all-purpose
Granulated sugar

Saucepan, 2-quart; pie pan, 9-inch; bowl, 2-quart

The night before baking, set the apple slices to soak in 2 cups of warm water in the saucepan.

Next day, prepare the pastry. Meanwhile simmer the apples in the saucepan until tender but not mushy. This will take about 20 to 30 minutes. Most of the liquid will boil away, but the slices should not lose their shape.

Preheat the oven to 425°F. Line the buttered pie pan with a bottom crust. In the bowl mix raisins, flour, and sugar. Spoon the stewed apples into the dry mixture and blend well. Any liquid remaining in the saucepan can go into your vinegar jug (see next recipe).

Fill the pie shell, cover with top crust, crimp, and vent. Bake at 425° for 15 minutes, then reduce heat to 350° and continue to bake until pie is nicely browned, about 40 minutes in all. Cool at least an hour before serving.

APPLE-CORE VINEGAR

> *Everything must be saved, nothing wasted of all the summer's bounty. Even the apple cores were saved for making vinegar. . . .*
> FARMER BOY

A quantity of good vinegar was important to a family that preserved its own meat and vegetables. What's more, vinegar was a common table garnish. The cruet was a fixture of the dinner table then as the catsup bottle is in diners today.

Since store products might contain dangerous acids, careful housewives made their own vinegar, taking pride in the special flavors they achieved. They began at preserving time with a clean barrel open at the top for air and receiving and fitted with a bung at the bottom for decanting. Into the barrel went rainwater, some of last year's vinegar, and the peel and cores from apple canning and drying. Sweetening might be added in the form of preserve-kettle skimmings, molasses-barrel rinsings, honey, or brown sugar. In time this mixture fermented, resembling hard cider or wine; in more time—several months—the ferment turned acid and became vinegar. In spring part of the batch might be moved to an outdoor barrel and mixed with rainwater and spices to become next season's pickling vinegar.

For your own batch you will have no vinegar "starter" or "mother," as Almanzo's family did, but never mind (store vinegar won't do; it's been pasteurized to kill essential bacteria). To encourage fermenting you may have to use baker's yeast rather than wait for the wild stuff to volunteer.

Once fermenting has started, it's best to add only fermented matter to the barrel. Thus, any leftovers from making jellies and jams (page 55), Apple Turnovers (page 122), or Dried Apple and Raisin Pie (page 130) should be saved in a separate container (glass is good) and put in the barrel only after they have gone through the bubbling stage.

Start your vinegarmaking as soon as the season's new apple crop is available so you can make several tries if necessary.

For $\frac{1}{2}$ gallon of cider vinegar you will need:
Spring, rain, or well water, $\frac{1}{2}$ gallon
Honey, 2 cups
Peels and cores of 12 or more apples
Dry yeast, $\frac{1}{2}$ package ($1\frac{1}{2}$ teaspoons) (optional)
Cider vinegar, $\frac{1}{2}$ cup commercial, for comparison only

Small barrel or plastic gallon jug; cork or lid; sipping straws

A fine stand-in for a barrel is a gallon plastic milk jug—the kind with a square base, self-handle, and narrow neck. It must be washed well and scalded. Find a place in the warm kitchen where it can rest on a side, with the narrow opening serving as a bunghole. Cut an opening on the top surface to receive a wide cork or plastic lid (the closing should not be airtight).

Boil the water, pour it in the jug, and stir in honey, peels, and cores. Cover, set aside, and check daily for bubbling. If none occurs in a week, add the yeast. If mold forms on the surface, skim it off without disturbing the contents.

After a month the bubbling will have stopped and souring begun. Now it is up to your taste to tell you when the vinegar is ready to use. To take a sample from the jug, plunge in a sipping straw, close the end with your thumb, and remove the straw half-full. Judge the strength by comparing with a taste of commercial vinegar.

In two months the vinegar may be sour enough to use in cooking and salad dressings. Try to decant a quantity from the bung without shaking up the contents. Replenish the barrel with any fermented matter on hand.

At some point a milky film may form on or below the surface of the vinegar in the barrel. This is a mother, a welcome sign of acetic acid bacteria but a possible nuisance. Best remove it, along with the other solid matter in the barrel.

Use your homemade product wherever vinegar is called for in this book *except* in pickling, which requires a vinegar of proven acidity. Recommended uses are on Fried Fish (page 44); with sugar on lettuce leaves (page 112); in Green Pumpkin Pie (page 120); in Ginger Water (page 185); and in Vinegar Pie (page 197).

Pickles and Picklemaking

Pickles have always had a special place on the table; even in today's varied diet they seem a treat. In Laura's youth they brought bright color, crisp texture, and tangy flavor to winter meals of mashed and stewed potatoes, squash, beans, and meat. Preserved cucumbers or "green pickles" were often the only touch of green on the table from October to May.

Pickles belonged to the bounty of the Wilder table. They were also part of the maple sugaring festivities in the Big Woods of Wisconsin. But not until the Ingallses finally settled on the Dakota claim did Ma again have the garden vegetables, the vinegar, and the containers to make her own.

Pickles are vegetables preserved in an acid solution strong enough to kill bacteria that cause spoiling. The oldest kind needed no container but a wooden barrel, where fresh cucumbers were put at harvest time in a mix of water, salt, vinegar, and spices called a brine. Kept submerged with a stone and stored in a cool cellar, the cucumbers fermented, gradually becoming stronger in flavor. Fetching pickles from cold brine in a dark cellar is a childhood memory rarely forgotten by those who did it.

Luckily Ma Ingalls lived during the canning revolution; she was able to seal her pickles in newly invented glass jars that kept them from becoming too strong or spoiling. She used a combination of old-fashioned brining and "open-kettle" canning that is still used today. Her green tomato pickles omitted the brining step entirely; they were fully cooked, just like preserves. So were Mother Wilder's beet pickles. Mother Wilder also made pickles of watermelon rind. In these days of watermelon bred with thin skins, recipes for this old favorite are more abundant than the prime ingredient.

What about pickling ingredients? The SALT was not—and should not be—"iodized" like modern table salt. Kosher salt is a good home substitute for coarse "pickling salt." The WATER was rain, well, or spring water, not the chlorinated water of modern city systems. City water can't spoil your pickling efforts, but some say it affects the taste.

As for VINEGAR, housewives in Laura's youth were urged to make their own and not rely on a store product that might turn out to be weak sulfuric acid. Protected against such frauds by the Pure Food and Drugs Act, we take the opposite view and recommend that you use commercial cider vinegar of reliable acidity.

Dill had not yet become the universal pickle FLAVOR in frontier days, but "whole pickling spices" could be bought as a mixture just as they are today. Such mixtures remain a convenient way to buy a wide variety of desirable flavors: cinnamon, allspice, coriander, mustard seed, bay leaves, ginger, chilies, cloves, black pepper, mace, and cardamom.

ALUM is a chemical powder long used in pickling as a "firming agent," to help some pickles retain crispness. Grape leaves were also used for this purpose. Neither is required for any of the recipes that follow.

For at least the last five generations, every new generation of picklemakers has been warned about proper *containers*. Copper vessels react chemically with vinegar solutions and must never be used. Enameled kettles are best for cooking acid solutions; before they were available, Ma and Mother Wilder may have used tin kettles. Pickles must never be stored in earthenware vessels that could impart lead. Before glass jars became abundant and cheap, wooden barrels and stoneware crocks were the recommended containers.

TOMATO PRESERVES

The sun was high now, all the frost was gone, and the wind was blowing cool over the brownish and purple and fawn-colored prairie. Ma and Laura picked the tomatoes. . . . There were enough ripe tomatoes to make almost a gallon of preserves.

THE LONG WINTER

The tomato is botanically a fruit, and it was often treated as such by nineteenth-century cooks, who served it and preserved it with sugar. Today we treat it as a vegetable, and surpluses end up as spaghetti sauce or relish more than as jam or marmalade.

This recipe, with many of the same ingredients, should appeal to ketchup lovers. It comes to us from Eliza Leslie, who warns, "The lemon must on no account be omitted." With the town nearby, Ma Ingalls may have had lemons on hand; then again, she may have "made do" with vinegar.

For four $\frac{1}{2}$ pints of preserves you will need:
Red ripe tomatoes, 2 pounds
Lemon, 1, or 2 tablespoons cider vinegar
Light-brown sugar, 2 pounds
Powdered ginger, $\frac{1}{4}$ teaspoon

Enameled kettle, 2- or 3-quart; lemon reamer; sterilizing kettle; $\frac{1}{2}$-pint canning jars, 4; ladle, tongs, and wide-mouthed funnel

Fill kettle with water and bring it to a boil. Loosen skins by dipping tomatoes in boiling water for half a minute. Peel and discard skins; cut up tomatoes. Empty kettle.

Squeeze lemon; reserve juice; score and shave off the peel. In the open kettle cook tomato pieces and sugar slowly until thick, stirring frequently. This may take more than an hour.

Add lemon juice and peel (or vinegar) and ginger. Cook another 30 minutes to the sheeting stage (page 57), skimming the surface of any white froth. Meanwhile sterilize jars (page 56). Using the funnel, ladle the thick pulp into hot jars and seal. When jars are cool, label and date and remove to cool dark shelves for at least two weeks.

BEET PICKLES

"At the edge of the plate he piled dark-red beet pickles."
That was Father Wilder's last gesture before handing to Almanzo
a Sunday dinner plate heaped with chicken pie, gravy, baked beans,
and salt pork. The pickles made it a feast for the eyes as well as the
palate.

"Pickled beets" are usually made by cooking and slicing
beets, then soaking them overnight in vinegar water for meals the
next day. But the term "beet pickles" refers to a product of home
canning, favored for its rich color as much as for its sweet/sour
flavor.

Small beets, four or five to the pound, make the nicest pickles, and buying them with stems and green tops (three pounds in
all) is one way to make sure they are not from cold storage.

For three pints you will need:
Beets, 2 pounds, trimmed of leaves
Granulated sugar, 1 cup
Cider vinegar, 1 cup
Salt, $\frac{1}{2}$ teaspoon
Pepper, a pinch
Whole cloves, 6

Enameled kettle or saucepan, 3-quart; 1-pint canning jars with
    lids, 3; sterilizing kettle; slotted spoon; ladle, tongs, and
    wide-mouth funnel

Trim beets and scrub them clean. Boil in kettle or saucepan in enough water to cover (2 to 3 cups) until beets are tender. This may take 20 to 40 minutes. Set beets aside to cool; pour away all but 1 cup of the liquid. Add to it sugar and vinegar; boil briskly until thickening starts, about 5 minutes.

Meanwhile skin beets with a table knife and cut crosswise in slices $\frac{1}{8}$ inch thick. Add slices, salt, and pepper to syrup and heat again, just to boiling. Sterilize canning jars (page 56). Using funnel and slotted spoon, transfer slices into jars. Add 2 cloves to each jar, ladle in hot liquid to fill jars, and seal. When they are cool, label and date jars and remove them to cool, dark shelf for at least two weeks.

GREEN CUCUMBER PICKLES

> *"Well, we've got good things to eat, and plenty of them," said Pa, taking a second helping of potatoes and peas.*
>
> *"Yes," Ma said happily; "nowadays we can all eat enough to make up for what we couldn't have last winter."*
>
> *She was proud of the garden; it was growing so well. "I shall begin salting down cucumbers tomorrow, little ones are thick under all those vines. And the potato tops are thriving so, I can hardly find the hills underneath them, to scrabble."*
>
> **LITTLE TOWN ON THE PRAIRIE**

"Salting down" is the first step in picklemaking. A large farm would have a barrel of brine in which each day's picking of cucumbers would be put to await a time convenient for picklemaking. Then the large ones might be sorted out to ferment naturally in a barrel or crock of cool brine, while the smaller ones would be "put up" in sealed jars.

To provide a sampling of old-fashioned dill-less pickles with the least fuss we have specified a small batch here and the minimum brine-curing time, 24 hours. In this method of pickling the "curing" continues in the jars, and a month on a cool shelf is required before the pickles are ready to eat.

Cucumbers for pickling should be small ones, fresh from a nearby garden or farm. At a store, ask for pickling cucumbers. Do not buy the large shiny ones that have been coated with wax for long-distance shipment.

For four 1-pint jars of pickles you will need:
Coarse salt, 1 cup
Fresh small cucumbers, 4 pounds
Cider vinegar, 3 cups
Brown sugar, 2 tablespoons
Mixed pickling spices, 1 full tablespoon

Enameled kettle, 6-quart or larger; sterilizing kettle; 1-pint canning jars with lids, 4; ladle, tongs and wide-mouth funnel

This is a two-day process. On the first day make a brine by heating 1 gallon of water to boiling in the enameled kettle. Add salt; remove from heat and stir until cool and clear.

Wash cucumbers, place them in the brine, and keep them submerged under a dinner plate or heavy lid. Cover all with a clean cloth and leave undisturbed at room temperature.

Next day pour off the brine. Rinse the cucumbers in fresh water and set them aside. Wash the preserving kettle. Sterilize the canning jars (page 56).

In the clean kettle boil 1 quart of water with the vinegar, brown sugar, and spices. Add cucumbers and simmer about 3 minutes. With tongs remove the cucumbers to the hot jars, packing them as closely as possible.

Ladle the simmering liquid into the jars until they are full. Jiggle contents slightly to release any lurking air bubbles. Cover and seal jars; wipe clean and label and date them. Store the cooled jars away from heat and light for a month before serving.

GREEN TOMATO PICKLES

Ma and Laura picked the tomatoes. The vines were wilted down, soft and blackening, so they picked even the smallest green tomatoes. There were enough ripe tomatoes to make almost a gallon of preserves.

"What are you going to do with the green ones?" Laura asked, and Ma answered, "Wait and see."

She washed them carefully without peeling them. She sliced them and cooked them with salt, pepper, vinegar, and spices.

"That's almost two quarts of green tomato pickle. Even if it's only our first garden on the sod and nothing could grow well, these pickles will be a treat with baked beans this winter," Ma gloated.

THE LONG WINTER

In climates where early frost often kills tomato vines still heavy with unripe tomatoes, home gardeners still turn to pickling to salvage their crop.

Our recipe follows the author's description to the letter, omitting the usual overnight brining and the onions and sugar found in most green tomato pickles. For spices we use the standard pickling mix (page 134).

For four 1-pint jars of pickles you will need:
Small green tomatoes, 5 pounds (about 22 tomatoes, $2\frac{1}{2}$ inches each)
Salt, 2 tablespoons
Mixed pickling spice, 3 tablespoons
Cider vinegar, 2 cups

Enameled kettle, 6-quart or larger; sterilizing kettle; 1-pint canning jars, with lids, 4; ladle, tongs, and wide-mouth funnel; slotted spoon

Wash the tomatoes well and divide them into six equal groups. Slice tomatoes in the first group crosswise, about $\frac{1}{4}$ inch thick, and arrange them in a layer covering the bottom of the enameled kettle. Sprinkle with a scant teaspoon of salt and $1\frac{1}{2}$ teaspoons of mixed spice. Repeat until you have six layers of tomatoes, salt, and spices. Pour in the vinegar and 2 cups of water slowly, without disturbing the layers, until the liquid reaches the top layer (add more water if needed to achieve this). Heat to boiling; reduce heat, and simmer uncovered about 15 minutes, or until a slice will cut easily with a fork.

Meanwhile sterilize jars (page 56).

If scum forms on bubbling surface of pickles skim it off with spoon edge. Using the funnel, with the slotted spoon fill the jars with slices and spices to within $\frac{1}{2}$ inch of the rims. Distribute the last spoonful with spice residue evenly among all jars. Ladle in liquid to fill. Apply lids and seal.

When jars are cool tighten lids, wipe jars clean, label and date, and store in cool dark place for at least two weeks.

Chapter
7

Foods from the Barnyard

THE DOG is the only animal domesticated by our native forebears. Indians before the white man ate meat with their corn, squash, and beans, but it was all from the wild—deer, bear, buffalo, squirrel, and the like. It was the European settlers who brought livestock and made barnyards a fixture of the American farm.

By the time Laura Ingalls was born only city people and very poor country folk lived without their own animals. For families like the Wilders, farm animals were the money crop, producing milk, eggs, and wool for sale. For frontier families like the Ingallses a few animals meant mobility, horsepower, and a reliable food source. Before the days of Crisco and corn oil, animals were not only a rich source of protein but the only source of fat, needed for energy and warmth. Prosperity in those days meant a full barnyard, and while the Ingallses never reached that exalted state they did have, by the time Laura married, at least six cows and heifers, a flock of chickens, and, of course, horses.

To keep animals took feed, shelter, and often fencing. A horse could feed on oats and hay in the barn through the winter and graze from a movable picket in the summer. Because it offered transportation and the power to pull stumps and draw a plow, it was usually the first animal acquired by the frontiersman.

To a family with young children a cow was next in importance, and the Ingallses managed to acquire one in almost every new
home. If twice-a-day milkings were begun as soon as the cow bore
a calf and became "fresh," she could produce enough milk through
the late spring, summer, and early fall to feed her calf and keep a
growing family in milk, butter, and cheese. When cold weather came
and fodder was less plentiful, the cow was allowed to go dry. If the
calf turned out to be a heifer, she was easily salable. A bull calf could
become a beef steer or a working ox.

Although they belonged to familiar breeds—probably Jersey
and Guernsey—the Ingallses' cows were different from their scien-

tifically bred descendants. A modern dairy cow can give eight times the quantity of milk expected from a cow of a century ago.

Raising cattle for beef had already become a business specialty, as we know from Pa's experience with the longhorn cattle in Kansas. The flat grasslands of Texas had proved ideal range country for the sturdy longhorn, brought to Mexico by the Spanish explorers. Traveling herders called "cowboys" drove them overland from Texas to markets and rail centers in the North. Between 1867 and 1890, Laura's birthdate and her twenty-third year, an estimated ten million head of longhorn made the long trip to market. In time meat producers found that young steers of Holstein, Angus, and other imported breeds could be fattened in feedlots and brought to butchering weight at half the age of their American cousins. With more fat in it, their meat was also more tender. As a result the longhorn population has dwindled to about 6,500 at this writing— some in a government refuge in Oklahoma, most in private herds in the West.

Pigs are still family farm favorites because they demand so little and offer so much. "Everything is useful," goes the saying, "but the squeal." A pig will eat anything people eat and much that we throw away. It will also eat grass and roots. At butchering time it will return a good share of its weight in usable meat and fat. In the Big Woods the pig must have been especially useful to a pioneer, plowing up and fertilizing the earth as it rooted in the wilds.

Pork, ham, spareribs, bacon, salt pork, headcheese, and lard —these are all gifts from the pig. How they tasted and appeared in Laura's youth we can only imagine, for all the swine now considered traditional American breeds have been developed since that time. That they were different from ours we can be sure, by contrasting the home-cured and commercially cured bacons of today or the hams of corn-fed hogs with those of peanut-fed hogs. One certainty is that our pigs are leaner than their forebears.

Chickens, too, have changed greatly. A poultry expert as well as an author, Laura Wilder lived to see poultry raising change from

a gentleman's sport and a farm wife's pocket money to two separate
giant industries, egg production and meat production. The scrawny
Leghorn, imported from Italy within the last century, is ancestor of
all modern "layers," while our "fryers" and "broilers" are American breeds raised on special feeds. With the Ingallses' flock it
worked this way:

> *If they could raise the chicks, if hawks or weasels or foxes did not
> get them, some would be pullets that summer. Next year the pullets
> would begin laying, then there would be eggs to set. Year after next,
> there would be cockerels to fry, and more pullets to increase the flock.
> Then there would be eggs to eat, and when the hens grew too old to lay
> eggs, Ma could make them into chicken pie.*

Not only were those chickens different from ours; their diet of grass
and insects and their long exposure to sunlight gave them a flavor
we cannot know from mass-production birds.

Today the automobile and tractor are our horsepower; the
dairy, beef, hog, and poultry industries have replaced the barnyard
as a source of America's favorite foods. Some things the barnyard
offered can never, however, be replaced by industry. For these we
turn to dogs, cats, canaries, hamsters, and fish—pets that give us the
companionship of animals and the satisfaction of nurturing living
beings.

Dairy "Products," Then and Now

Milk, the saying goes, is the perfect food for calves, infants, and bacteria. In its use as human food it has often served as well as a carrier of disease. Ma Ingalls and Mother Wilder knew that new milk would sour or their families might get sick if they neglected to keep cows and milking equipment absolutely clean. Milk pans should not have seams where dirt could gather, and they had to be scalded with each use.

It was not until after Laura's birth that pioneering European doctors and chemists established that both infections in animals and the souring and fermenting of food are caused by living cells too small to be seen—microbes, bacteria, germs. These germs, they also found, could not survive high heat.

For this reason the milk we buy in the store today has all been heat-treated to kill germs that might spread disease. We call the process pasteurization in honor of Louis Pasteur, one of the discoverers of microbes.

Pasteurization also kills the germs that cause fermenting and give milk its "sour power." There are many such germs. One type turns milk to yogurt; others account for certain varieties of cheese.

Over the years these useful germs have been sorted out in laboratories and grown in safe isolation, or cultured. Modern dairies add cultured ferments to pasteurized milk to produce modern yogurt, sour cream, and commercial buttermilk. Because of culturing, dairy buttermilk looks and tastes different from what you will get by making butter from pasteurized cream, but it will perform in recipes the way old-fashioned raw buttermilk did. It is also an excellent substitute for raw sour milk, furnishing the acid often needed to react with baking soda. Because it is more widely available than raw milk, we have used it throughout this book.

LARD AND CRACKLINGS

> *All that day and the next, Ma was trying out the lard in big iron*
> *pots on the cookstove. Laura and Mary carried wood and watched the*
> *fire. It must be hot, but not too hot, or the lard would burn. The big*
> *pots simmered and boiled, but they must not smoke. From time to time*
> *Ma skimmed out the brown cracklings. She put them in a cloth and*
> *squeezed out every bit of the lard, and then she put the cracklings away.*
> *She would use them to flavor johnny-cake later.*
>
> *Cracklings were very good to eat, but Laura and Mary could have*
> *only a taste. They were too rich for little girls, Ma said.*
>
> **LITTLE HOUSE IN THE BIG WOODS**

All those salty, fatty, crispy snacks that adults eat at parties and children nibble the rest of the time are not a far cry from cracklings, the crunchy brown remains of pork fat after the lard has been cooked out.

Cracklings are somewhat hazardous to make, and some mothers still think them hazardous for children to eat, so you may have to bargain with the head cook. Promise that if you get help with this effort, you will make cracklings the next time a large ham is bought for a party (cracklings from ham fat, being already smoked and salted, are really good).

Any butcher will probably give you all the pork fat you want. We used the fat from an untrimmed pork roast of about five pounds to test this recipe. As you increase the amount of fat, you must, of course, also increase the size of your kettle and the number of lard containers.

Ma would have put her lard in stoneware jars, covered them with cloth, and stored them in a cool place. Even if you don't plan to save the lard for deep-fat frying or for pie paste, do pour it into a small container to harden and not down the drain.

For ½ cup of cracklings and 1 scant cup of lard you will need:
Fresh pork fat, about ½ pound

Kettle with lip and cover, 6-cup; small baking pan; cheesecloth; slotted spoon; 6-ounce jar with tight lid

Watch out for two dangers. One is burning yourself. Wear an apron; have hotpads available for all operations. The other is burning the lard and cracklings by having the fat too hot. "A moment's neglect will ruin all."

Cube the fat and put in kettle with ½ cup of water. Heat to boiling, cover, then reduce heat to simmer. You may do other kitchen chores for the first 30 minutes.

After about a half-hour, when the water has cooked away, remove lid and raise temperature slightly. Prepare to watch and stir frequently for the next half-hour or so. The fat cubes will gradually shrivel and brown, but the fat should remain clear. If fat starts to brown, reduce heat. Scrape particles off bottom as you stir.

Line the baking pan with a square of cheesecloth. As the fat pieces brown, they will rise, then sink to the bottom. Remove them to the cloth with the slotted spoon. When only fine particles are left, remove fat from heat.

Carefully gather up the cheesecloth, press it with the spoon against the side of the kettle to drain the last fat, and empty cracklings into jar. Return cheesecloth to baking pan and carefully pour hot fat in. If there are pieces worth saving, repeat squeezing operation. Discard cheesecloth.

Chill the lard until firm, then remove from pan and wrap for refrigerator storage or disposal. For snacking, fresh cracklings are best. To use later for Crackling Cornbread (page 25), cover tightly and store in cool cupboard, not the refrigerator.

BAKED SPARERIBS

Carrie could remember butchering time, but Grace had never held a pig's skinned tail in front of the cookstove grate and watched it sizzling brown. She had never seen Ma take from the oven the dripping pan full of brown, crackling, juicy spareribs.

LITTLE TOWN ON THE PRAIRIE

When you eat a loin pork chop—one of the best cuts a pig can offer—you are eating the meat attached to a rib where it joins the chine, or backbone. When you eat spareribs (spare of meat), you are eating what is left of the ribs after the loin has been cut away. Spareribs are close to the fat belly of the pig; they are not far from the portions that yield bacon and salt pork.

In our time spareribs have become a vehicle for all kinds of spicy-sweet barbecue sauces. They are a staple of take-out Chinese food services. Yet they really can be tasty without any garnish at all —which is how they were probably served on butchering day, when no one had time to fuss. The key is to bake them not just until the meat is "done," but until most of the fat is rendered out—in a moderate oven, at least two hours. For the first hour they will produce a clear fat that can be drained and chilled for drippings.

Baked Hubbard Squash (page 114), which takes about the same amount of oven time, makes an excellent complement.

For six servings you will need:
Pork spareribs, 5 to 6 pounds
Salt and pepper

Dripping pans, 2; container for fat

Preheat oven to 350°F and arrange shelves to accommodate two pans.

Rinse the ribs and pat them dry. Cut them into individual portions of 3 to 4 ribs. Salt and pepper them and arrange in pans.

Bake in moderate oven for 1 hour. Spoon the fat out of the pans, turn the ribs, and bake until brown and crackling, at least another hour.

HOMEMADE SAUSAGE

The little pieces of meat, lean and fat, that had been cut off the large pieces, Ma chopped and chopped until it was all chopped fine. She seasoned it with salt and pepper and with dried sage leaves from the garden. Then with her hands she tossed and turned it until it was well mixed, and she molded it into balls. She put the balls in a pan out in the shed, where they would freeze and be good to eat all winter. That was the sausage.

LITTLE HOUSE IN THE BIG WOODS

When Mother Wilder made sausage she had the help of a grinder and a son to operate it. Ma Ingalls had neither; but then, she had but one pig to care for at butchering time. Both cooks had the advantage of a freezing climate to preserve their meat in cakes. In a warmer climate, one had the added chores of scraping the intestines for casings; of stuffing the delicate casings without bubbling or bursting; and of packing them in brine or hanging them in the smokehouse or both.

This mixture is called country sausage today, although "porkburger" would suit it as well, since the ratio of lean to fat is the same as in the typical beefburger. There is no better recipe to demonstrate the relation of texture and flavor: you will find your hand-chopped sausage worlds away from the commercial product of high-speed grinders, even though the ingredients are the same.

To make country sausage without butchering, ask a butcher for quantities of lean and fat pork, or buy a loin or shoulder of four pounds or more and cut it apart yourself.

For six servings of country sausage you will need:
Pork, 2 pounds lean and 1 pound fat
Salt, 1 tablespoon
Pepper, 1 teaspoon
Dried sage, 1 tablespoon crumbled

Boning knife; chopper and bowl; bowl, 2-quart; bowl, 3-quart; freezer wrap; skillet, 12-inch

Separate the lean and fat pork, using boning knife; cut both into 1-inch cubes. (Use bones for soup stock.) Keeping in mind the old slogan "blade sharp; meat cool," sharpen your chopper and start to mince the cubes a few at a time. Put chopped fat in smaller bowl and chopped lean in larger one. Keep the bowl you're not working on and unchopped cubes covered in refrigerator.

In the large bowl combine choppings, adding one part fat for every two parts of lean. Add seasoning. With hands that have been washed with unscented soap blend the sausage and shape it in individual patties to freeze or to fry immediately.

To serve for breakfast, thaw frozen sausage in refrigerator overnight. *Do not* attempt to thaw or to cook by parboiling or you will have hard, flavorless cakes.

Brown sausage cakes in skillet for 4 to 6 minutes over medium-high heat. Turn and brown the other side. Lower the heat, cover the pan, and cook the cakes through for 15 to 20 minutes more. Pork should always be well cooked. Remove cakes to a warm platter.

For gravy, beat 2 tablespoons flour into 1 cup milk. Pour into the skillet over low heat and stir until it is thick and bubbly and the pan is scraped clean. Taste and correct seasoning. Almanzo's mother would have poured the gravy right over the sausage cakes on the big blue platter, but we advise you to serve the gravy separately. Although this lean sausage is well suited to modern tastes, the fat gravy may not be.

ROASTED PIG

Almanzo bowed his head and shut his eyes tight while Father said the blessing. It was a long blessing, because this was Christmas Day. But at last Almanzo could open his eyes. He sat and silently looked at that table.

He looked at the crisp, crackling little pig lying on the blue platter with an apple in its mouth. He looked at the fat roast goose, the drumsticks sticking up, and the edges of dressing curling out. The sound of Father's knife sharpening on the whetstone made him even hungrier.

FARMER BOY

Since the olden days of Almanzo's youth ovens have gotten smaller and pigs, on average, have gotten larger. This means you are not likely to find a pig you can stretch out straight and roast slowly overnight. A commercially raised suckling pig, 12 to 25 pounds, must be doubled over to fit an 18-inch oven and turned during roasting, so you can't sleep while it cooks or display it in the traditional pose, prone on a platter with an apple in its mouth. It is still worth doing.

Pork should always be well done. This is easy to do with the fast-cooking well-lubricated flesh of a young porker. At moderate temperature, 350°F, an 18-pound suckling pig, stuffed, will be done in four hours. It will feed up to fourteen people. Handling it in the kitchen will take two pairs of hands.

You will need:

A dressed suckling pig, 15 to 20 pounds, with haslets (see below)

Stale light bread, 2 pounds sliced (8 to 10 cups coarse crumbs)

Yellow onions, 1 pound

Butter, 5 tablespoons

Dried sage, 2 to 3 tablespoons crumbled

Eggs, 2

Cider, 1 cup

Parsley, $\frac{1}{2}$ cup chopped fresh

Ground nutmeg and mace, generous pinches

White flour, 2 tablespoons unbleached all-purpose

Cranberries, $\frac{1}{2}$ cup whole

Small red apple

Garnish: parsley, cress, celery leaves, or evergreen boughs

Dripping pan, 6-quart, or large roaster; saucepan, 1-quart; chopper and bowl; skillet, 10-inch; bowl, 6-quart; bowl, 1-quart; skewers and lacing thread; wooden block or empty tomato paste can; needle and heavy thread; large platter or carving board

Take with you to the butcher shop the dripping pan or the largest roaster your oven will hold. Ask the butcher to lace the snout and feet with string so the pig can be tied up to fit the pan. The pig should have clean ears, be free of hair, and be accompanied by haslets or organs—liver, heart, and lungs.

Back home, rinse the pig inside and out with cold water and pat dry. Keep it cold while preparing broth and stuffing.

To make gravy broth, simmer haslets in 2 cups of water in saucepan. After about 20 minutes' cooking, the large, strongly flavored liver can be removed and chopped fine to add to the stuffing. A little later, set aside the heart and lungs as Christmas dinner for the cat.

To prepare stuffing, put dry bread crumbs or slices in a dishtowel and pound them into fine crumbs with a mallet or rolling pin. Peel and chop onions coarsely and fry in skillet until limp in 3 tablespoons of the butter. Combine crumbs, onions, and sage in large bowl.

In small bowl beat eggs and stir in cider. Add chopped parsley, nutmeg, and mace, and blend into crumb mixture. Stir in chopped liver if you wish. Preheat oven to 350°F.

Spoon the stuffing loosely into the pig's cavity and close the opening with skewers and lacing. Draw the head and back feet together with the butcher's string and tie it. Place the pig in the dripping pan or roaster, and rub all skin surfaces generously with remaining butter. With a sharp knife slash the back skin in several places to permit fat to escape. Use wood block or small can to prop mouth open during roasting. Add 1 cup of boiling water to pan and place pig and pan in preheated oven.

After an hour baste pig with pan juices. In another 30 minutes check for browning: when top side is thoroughly browned, turn pig over (a two-person job) and continue roasting. The pig is done when fully browned and when skin begins to shrink and break.

While the pig is roasting, chill the haslet broth and remove fat from the surface. Blend flour into the broth. Using needle and thread, string a cranberry necklace for decoration.

At serving time remove pig to large platter or board and cut away string. If suitable for display, tie on cranberry necklace and place cranberries in eye sockets. Replace mouth prop with apple. Garnish platter with greens.

Skim pan gravy of excess fat and stir in floured broth. Heat and stir until gravy is thick and smooth. Season to taste and transfer to gravy bowl.

At the table, start carving by cutting off the pig's head. Next run the knife down the spine and lay the body open in two halves. From this point the division of portions—shoulders, ribs, hams, etc. —becomes self-evident.

MINCEMEAT; MINCE PIE

Next Mother made mincemeat. She boiled the best bits of beef and
pork and chopped them fine. She mixed in raisins and spices, sugar and
vinegar, chopped apples and brandy, and she packed two big jars full
of mincemeat. It smelled delicious, and she let Almanzo eat the scraps
left in the mixing bowl.

FARMER BOY

Centuries ago, while American Indians were making pemmi-
can of dried chopped meat, fat, and berries, our European forebears
were preserving a similar mixture as "mincemeat." At butchering
time the odd bits of head meat and tongue were extended with fresh
apples, dried fruits, and spices and preserved in liquor. Some of the
hard fat surrounding the beef kidneys, called suet, was also included
(the pork fat became lard). In lean times the mixture might be made
without any meat at all.

Old American mincemeat recipes reflect a land rich first in
venison and later in beef. The preparations now available in jars and
dehydrated packages are usually faithful to traditional ingredients
but finely textured and cooked to a syrupy state. Cooking only the
meat and chopping all by hand will give you the experience of
mincemeat at its old-fashioned best.

In place of "two big jars" we recommend four smaller ones
that hold enough for one pie each.

For four $1\frac{1}{2}$-pint jars you will need:
Beef, $1\frac{1}{2}$ pounds neck or other bony cut
Pork, 1 pound rib ends or other bony cut
Salt and pepper, generous pinches
Lemon, 1
Orange, 1
Tart apples, 2 pounds (about 8 greenings or pippins)
White suet, $\frac{1}{2}$ pound
Brown sugar, $1\frac{1}{2}$ cups
Maple flavoring, $\frac{1}{2}$ teaspoon
Cider vinegar, $\frac{2}{3}$ cup

Ground cloves, cinnamon, and nutmeg, 1 teaspoon each, or 2
    teaspoons pumpkin pie spice
Dark raisins, $\frac{2}{3}$ pound
Currants, $\frac{1}{2}$ pound
Brandy, $\frac{3}{4}$ cup

Kettle, with lid, 8-quart; chopper and bowl; bowl, 6-quart;
    bowl, 2-quart; sterilizing kettle; $1\frac{1}{2}$-pint canning jars, with
    lids, 4; ladle, tongs, and wide-mouth funnel

In covered kettle simmer meat and bones in 2 cups of water for 30 minutes. Remove lid, add salt and pepper, and continue to simmer at least another 30 minutes, until liquid reduces to 1 cup.

Meanwhile slice and chop lemon and orange. Peel, core, slice, and chop apples, and toss them with lemon and orange in large bowl. Cube, then mince, the suet and add it to the mixture.

Remove meat and bones to small bowl to cool. To the kettle broth add brown sugar, maple flavor, vinegar, and spices, and boil for a minute or two. Remove from heat and add raisins and currants to soak while you prepare meat and jars.

Sterilize jars (page 56). Pick meat from bones and chop it fine (discard bones). Add meat to kettle along with apple-citrus-suet mixture and boil for 5 minutes, stirring to prevent scorching.

Using funnel, ladle the mincemeat into hot sterilized jars, add 3 tablespoons of brandy to each, and seal. When the jars are cool, invert them several times to blend contents, label them, and remove to a cool, dark, dry shelf. The mincemeat may be used immediately, but a month's aging improves the flavor.

TO MAKE MINCE PIE

Preheat the oven to 425°F. Line a 9-inch buttered pie plate with Common Family Paste for Pies (page 194). Fill the crust with $1\frac{1}{2}$ pints cool mincemeat. Prepare a top crust of same pie paste or Fine Pie Paste (page 196) and cover the pie, crimping and venting to finish.

Bake the pie at 425° for 10 minutes, then reduce heat to 350° and continue baking another 30 minutes or until crust is golden brown. Serve warm with sweetened whipped cream.

POACHED FRESH EGGS

> *Supper was ready when Pa came from the stable and Laura had strained the milk.*
>
> *It was a happy family, all together again, as they ate of the browned hashed potatoes, poached fresh eggs and delicious biscuit with Ma's good butter. Pa and Ma drank their fragrant tea, but Mary drank milk with the other girls. "It is a treat," she said. "We don't have such good milk at college."*
>
> THESE HAPPY GOLDEN YEARS

Eggs for the Ingallses were seasonal but unquestionably fresh; for us, they are abundant year-round but rarely barnyard fresh. On the whole we are better off, except when we want eggs poached the old-fashioned way, without special appliances. For this eggs must be freshly laid.

In Laura's time farm hens stopped laying during winter months; a new nest of eggs was a sure sign of spring. Surplus summer eggs were greased and packed in bran for storage or preserved in crocks of brine, slaked lime, or waterglass, a chemical solution.

Now there are factorylike henhouses lighted like a summer day, hybridized hens, vitamin supplements, and other techniques to assure us a steady supply of layers and eggs. But they are often far from our table, and shipping reduces freshness. For most uses it doesn't matter, and federal and state grading standards protect us from stale or harmful produce. For poaching we must seek out the freshest eggs available.

If there's no nearby henhouse where you can buy same-day eggs, look in the store for eggs from a ranch or farm close to home —eggs that would not have aged in shipping. On shipped cartons look for the U.S.D.A. shield and the label Grade A or AA. There will be a date stamp indicating the last allowable date of sale; make sure it is at least a week in the future.

Once home with your eggs and ready to cook, make a final test by breaking eggs into saucers. If they sit in neat mounds, like yolks upon cushions, they are fresh enough to poach as follows. If they spread out in all directions or have broken yolks you'd better scramble them instead.

For six servings you will need:
Fresh eggs, 6

Skillet, 12-inch; saucers, 3; slotted spoon

Start by preparing any accompaniments—hash-browns, biscuits, or toast. Warm plates. Put 1 inch of water in the skillet and bring it to a boil. Break three eggs into saucers. Remove skillet from heat and slip eggs one by one into the water. Let them stand until the clear parts whiten and set. Return pan to heat and boil once again. A second or two of boiling should cloud over the yolk and complete the cooking. The yolk should remain fluid.

Remove eggs with slotted spoon to a warm plate. Rinse the skillet, add fresh water, and poach the remaining eggs.

FRIED CHICKEN

The fried chicken dinner served with the first peas and new potatoes of July during Laura's "happy golden years" on the claim shows a southern influence in Ma's cooking, for northerners had not yet embraced this now universal style of preparing spring chickens. Like the vegetables, the birds would have been young (about sixteen weeks) and tender. Today we speak instead of "fryers," hybridized fowl that reach cooking weight in half the time on a diet of appetite stimulants and enriched feed. Some say these streamlined fryers have less flavor than their barnyard forebears. Perhaps that is why they are so often cooked in seasoned, sweetened coatings!

The acid-salt-water bath, originally a butchering practice, seems to contribute to flavor and crispness in this recipe. A good substitute for homemade vinegar is the juice of a lemon.

For six small servings you will need:
A frying chicken, 3 to 3½ pounds, cut into serving pieces
Salt
Cider vinegar, 2 tablespoons
White flour, ⅔ cup unbleached all-purpose
Butter, 4 heaping tablespoons
Lard, 4 heaping tablespoons

Bowl, 2-quart; pie pan; skillet, 12-inch; tongs; heatproof platter; container for leftover fat

At least an hour before serving put chicken pieces in bowl, sprinkle with 1 tablespoon of salt and the vinegar, and cover with very cold water. Let stand for 30 minutes or more.

Strew flour in pie pan. Drain chicken, shake off each piece, and roll it in flour. In the skillet heat and blend the butter and lard.

When fat is hot but not smoking use tongs to put in dredged pieces. Take great care, as the meeting of moisture and hot fat causes sputtering.

Start warming a platter. With skillet on medium-high heat brown chicken thoroughly, about 5 minutes to a side. Reduce heat to medium-low and cook 10 to 15 minutes longer, until fork-tender. The cooking can also be completed in a moderate oven. Remove chicken to the warm platter and serve.

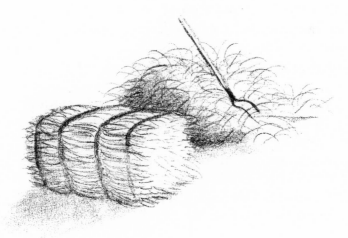

CHICKEN PIE

Mother was in the pantry, setting the top crust on the Sunday chicken pie. Three fat hens were in the pie, under the bubbling gravy. Mother spread the crust and crimped the edges, and the gravy showed through the two pine-trees she had cut in the dough. She put the pie in the heating-stove's oven, with the beans and rye'n'injun bread. Father filled the stove with hickory logs and closed the dampers, while Mother flew to lay out his clothes and dress herself.

FARMER BOY

The very thought of a three-hen pie seems to have addled the author! The crust Mother Wilder made above is clearly pie paste. Yet later, at the table, the description sounds more like biscuit dough, as Father "scooped out big pieces of thick crust and turned up their fluffy yellow undersides on the plate." Both coverings were popular for chicken pie at the time; often there was also a thick, soggy bottom crust as well. We tested both and found that only piecrust survives slow baking for four or more hours (the time it took, after Sunday breakfast, to dress, drive an hour's round trip to church, and sit through a two-hour sermon).

One hen is just enough for six people providing it is a roaster (4 to 5 months old) or a stewing hen (over a year old). Not only are these older birds larger than fryers; they are also more flavorful, especially when simmered in their skins. They are sometimes hard to find fresh in supermarkets.

Traditional chicken pies might differ in their crusts, but they almost always contained hard-boiled eggs.

For six servings you will need:

A roasting or stewing hen, about 5 pounds, cut into serving
    pieces
Common Family Paste for Pies (page 194)
Eggs, 3 hard-boiled
Bacon, 3 slices
Flour, 2 tablespoons
Salt and pepper

Saucepan, 1-quart; skillet, 12-inch; baking dish, 2-quart

Roasters and stewing chickens are usually sold whole. If the butcher cuts yours up, be sure he gives you the backbone and giblets.

Start preparing six hours before serving. Put giblets and backbone in 2 cups of boiling water in saucepan and simmer uncovered about 30 minutes.

Prepare and refrigerate a piecrust large enough to cover the baking dish with a 1-inch margin all around.

Preheat oven to 250°F. While pie dough chills, fry bacon in skillet until crisp and remove it to drain. Brown chicken in hot fat on all sides. Remove pieces to baking dish, grouping white meat on one side and dark meat on the other. Arrange the pieces in a mound so they will support the top crust evenly. Slice eggs and crumble bacon; strew eggs and bacon on chicken.

Pour off most of the fat in the skillet. Stir in the flour. Mash and blend in the liver from the saucepan. Pour in the saucepan liquid and stir well, returning to heat just until it bubbles.

Salt and pepper this gravy to taste, and pour it over the chicken and garnishes. Place piecrust loosely on top so it slumps inside the rim of the dish. Vent the top with two different pine tree designs to distinguish the light meat side from the dark. Crimp the crust edge around the rim. Bake for $4\frac{1}{2}$ to 5 hours.

STUFFED ROASTED HEN

> *In the morning, there would be all the surprises from the stockings, and at noon there would be the special Christmas feast, with a big fat hen stuffed and roasted, brown and juicy, and Almanzo would be there, for Ma had asked him to Christmas dinner. The wind was blowing hard, but it had not the shriek and howl of a blizzard wind, so probably he would be able to come tomorrow.*
>
> *"Oh, Laura!" Carrie said, as Laura blew out the lamp in the bedroom. "Isn't this the nicest Christmas! Do Christmases get better all the time?"*
>
> *"Yes," Laura said. "They do."*
>
> THESE HAPPY GOLDEN YEARS

A big fat hen is not so easy to find these days, when most roasting chickens in the market weigh five to six pounds. Poultry raisers like the Ingallses would have chosen a hen from their flock who showed more talent for fattening than for laying, possibly reaching eight or nine pounds.

The old custom of coating a roasting bird with flour, or dredging it, is recalled here. The stuffing is one that "will separate like rice when served," as the old standard goes. Notice that it uses butter instead of salt pork and two different herbs—marks of a full barnyard and a successful kitchen garden. Christmases had indeed improved for the Ingallses!

For six servings you will need:
Butter, $\frac{1}{2}$ cup for stuffing, plus 1 tablespoon for bird
A roasting chicken, 5 to 7 pounds
Light bread, 1 pound dried
Salt
Pepper, $\frac{1}{4}$ teaspoon
Dried sage, 1 tablespoon crumbled
Dried savory, 1 tablespoon crumbled
White flour, unbleached all-purpose

Dripping pan; saucepan, 1-quart; cheese grater or towel and
    rolling pin; bowl, 3-quart; needle and thread or skewers;
    small baking dish

Melt $\frac{1}{2}$ cup of butter in dripping pan in oven as it heats to
325°F. For gravy, simmer giblets and neck in saucepan with 3 cups
of water.

For stuffing, make bread crumbs by grating dry bread or by
rolling pieces in a folded towel with a rolling pin. Toss well in bowl
with the melted butter, and mix in 1 teaspoon of salt, the pepper,
sage, and savory.

Wash and dry the hen and rub the cavities with salt. Fill them
loosely with stuffing. Close the openings, neck and abdomen, with
stitches or skewers. Tuck wings behind nape of neck. If there is
stuffing remaining, put it in a greased baking dish and sprinkle with
some water (about $\frac{1}{4}$ cup).

Butter the skin of the hen, then dust it with salt and flour.
Place it in the dripping pan breast down and roast in oven for 1
hour, then turn the hen carefully on its back. If the breast is dry rub
it again with butter, dust with flour, and return to oven.

Check the simmering giblets: when the liquid has reduced by
half remove from heat. Discard the neck; chop giblets fine for gravy
or cut up to give to animals.

After another 40 minutes check the hen. If it is not browning
coat the skin with grease skimmed from the gravy broth. The hen
will be done when the skin is brown and the legs move easily—this
may take up to 3 hours.

Remove roast to a warm serving platter while you make the
gravy. Stir 2 tablespoons of flour into the dripping pan. Heat the
pan as you gradually stir in the giblet broth. Stir constantly until
the gravy thickens, scraping the pan clean as you do. Pour it into a
serving bowl.

Spoon the extra stuffing onto the platter and serve.

ROASTED STUFFED GOOSE

The turkey and ham that have become Christmas dinner standards in America undoubtedly are substitutes for goose and suckling pig, traditional European dishes that were—and are— served by families able to find and afford them.

That the Wilders had both suckling pig and goose on their Christmas table says something about their prosperity and heritage. It surely impressed Laura Wilder when years later, in her recital of savory details, she conjured up a "fat roast goose, the drumsticks sticking up." "The white breast of the goose," she noted, "went piece by piece from the bare breast-bone." In truth, geese, whether wild or domestic, are all dark meat, and their tiny legs would scarcely make impressive drumsticks!

We think the Wilder goose came from the farm flock, a source of meat, quality fat, and featherbed down. It is a bird well suited to overnight roasting, as Mother Wilder did it, since the dark meat needs long cooking and the fatty underskin acts as a self-basting agent. Mashed potatoes were the customary stuffing and apples the traditional accompaniment, whether baked, sauced, or fried with onions.

The size of your goose will depend on where you get it. Frozen ones offered by supermarkets are usually ten or eleven pounds; home fanciers often offer them smaller and younger. The timing for cooking is the same for all sizes.

For six servings (minimum) you will need:
A dressed goose, $6\frac{1}{2}$ to 12 pounds
Butter, 2 tablespoons
Potatoes, 10 medium
Onions, 2 medium
White flour, $\frac{1}{3}$ cup unbleached all-purpose
Egg, 1 beaten
Milk, $1\frac{1}{2}$ cups
Salt
Pepper
Dried sage, 1 tablespoon crumbled

Dried parsley, 1 tablespoon crumbled

Dried thyme, 1 tablespoon crumbled

Saucepan, 2-quart; skillet, 10-inch; saucepan for potatoes; bowl, 3-quart; chopper and bowl; small bowl; needle and heavy thread, or 2 skewers; baking dish, 1-quart; dripping pan, 6-quart; crock or tin for fat

If the goose is frozen set it out in the morning of the day before you plan to eat it to thaw at room temperature. When thawed, remove giblets (except liver) to 2-quart saucepan and simmer them in 3 cups of water.

Fry liver for a few minutes in skillet with 1 tablespoon of butter. Remove liver and save; set skillet aside for later use.

To prepare stuffing, boil and skin the potatoes and mash them coarsely in the 3-quart bowl. Chop onions fine and cook them in skillet in remaining butter until wilted. In small bowl blend $\frac{1}{4}$ cup flour with beaten egg; mix in larger bowl with potatoes. Add onion and butter, milk, 1 teaspoon of salt, pepper to taste, and herbs, and mix well. Spoon the stuffing into the main and neck cavities of the rinsed goose and close with needle and thread or skewers. Excess stuffing may be put in buttered baking dish. Place bird breast up in dripping pan. Brush stuffing in dish with milk and place it and goose in oven at 165°F for about 8 hours.

When simmering liquid with giblets has reduced by half remove from heat. Cut up heart and gizzard for pets. Chill broth and liver while goose roasts, then remove fat from broth.

Eight hours after starting, test the goose for doneness by trying to move its leg back and forth. Repeat every 30 minutes until the leg moves freely in its socket. In 10 hours the goose should certainly be done.

Remove goose to heated platter. Pour clear pan fat (there will be lots of it) into crock or jar without disturbing particles in pan. Mash liver in pan, add remaining flour, and blend with pan matter. Stir in giblet broth, heating pan as you do. When liquid boils and thickens, season it to taste and pour it into a warm serving bowl.

Spoon excess stuffing around goose on platter and serve.

BUTTER

For both Laura Wilder and her husband the regular churning of cream into butter was a vivid childhood memory. *Little House in the Big Woods* describes in detail winter Thursdays when Ma warmed the cream in the tall crockery churn, added carrot coloring, and moved the scalded dasher in it until tiny grains of yellow butter formed. *Farmer Boy* recalls buttermaking on a grander scale—twice-a-week churnings in a rocker-mounted barrel until there were five hundred pounds in butter tubs in the cellar to be sold to a New York buyer.

Even in those days, when fifty cents would buy a lace blouse or cousin Frank's plaid cap with ear-flaps, Mother Wilder's butter commanded fifty cents a pound. Why? Partly because she churned twice a week before the cream soured and because she took great care with the implements, scalding before each use. Partly because she had a large cool cellar for storage. But mostly because, as the author wrote, "she washed every bit of buttermilk out of it." Squeezing out all the liquid is the key to quality butter, and it was not easy in the days before mechanical butter "workers."

Mother Wilder's achievement is hard for us to appreciate in a time when science, industry, and the law have made quality butter a commonplace. We know little of the experience that made the eminent Catharine Beecher write, over a century ago,

America must have the credit of manufacturing and putting into market more bad butter than all that is made in all the rest of the world together. The varieties of bad tastes and smells which prevail in it are quite a study. This has a cheesy taste, that a mouldy, this is flavored with cabbage, and that again with turnip, and another has the strong, sharp savor of rancid animal fat. These varieties probably come from the practice of churning only at long intervals, and keeping the cream meanwhile in unventilated cellars or dairies, the air of which is loaded with the effluvia of vegetable substances. . . .

To make butter with a churn, either the standing kind like Ma's or a tabletop jar-mounted model, simply follow the description in Chapter 2 of *Big Woods*. The recipe below is for those who want to make a small quantity using only a canning jar. Working with a partner will make it go easier and faster.

For ½ pound of butter you will need:
Carrot, 1 medium
Homogenized milk, ¼ cup
Heavy whipping cream, 3 cups chilled
Salt, a pinch

Grater; saucepan, 1-pint; jar or container with tight lid, 2-quart;
    fine strainer; bowl, 2-quart; buttermold or small serving
    dish

Prepare coloring by grating carrot and heating it with milk in
saucepan. Scald all remaining equipment—jar, lid, strainer, bowl,
mold, and a wooden spoon. Rinse and chill with cold water.
    Strain warm tinted milk into jar. Add cream from refrigerator
and fasten lid. Shake jar a minute; open lid to release gas, and

refasten. Continue shaking, alternating with a partner.

In about 15 minutes the contents will form a thick mush. Continue shaking until contents resembles wheat grains floating in milk (the time will vary with the age of the cream, its temperature, and your shaking style).

Pour contents through strainer into bowl. Empty the milk from the bowl into another container. Turn the butter back into the bowl and cover with cold water. Stir well; strain off and discard water. Repeat washings until water is clear.

With the back of a wooden spoon work the liquid out of the butter by stirring and pressing it against the bowl. Dividing the butter and working half at a time makes it easier. When all liquid has been freed and poured off, work in a little salt, then press butter into mold or dish. Rinse with cold water and chill. Serve later with homemade bread, unmolding if necessary.

COTTAGE CHEESE BALLS

> "... I do know this, Caroline," he said. "No pesky mess of grasshoppers can beat us! We'll do something! You'll see! We'll get along somehow."
>
> "Yes, Charles," said Ma.
>
> "Why not?" said Pa. "We're healthy, we've got a roof over our heads; we're better off than lots of folks. You get an early dinner, Caroline. I'm going to town. I'll find something to do. Don't you worry!"
>
> While he was gone to town, Ma and Mary and Laura planned a fine supper for him. Ma scalded a pan of sour milk and made pretty white balls of cottage cheese. Mary and Laura sliced cold boiled potatoes and Ma made a sauce for them. There were bread and butter and milk besides.
>
> ON THE BANKS OF PLUM CREEK

Cottage cheese, also known as pot cheese and farmer cheese, is made with skim milk.

As the story suggests, cottage cheese can be made fairly quickly, but only after the milk has soured. That may take several days, depending on the age and temperature of the milk. To assure proper souring of pasteurized milk you must add some cultured buttermilk.

Only small-curd cottage cheese can be made by the method described here. Large-curd cottage cheese requires rennet and the special curd-cutting procedure involved in making Hard Cheese (following recipe).

For a dozen cottage cheese balls (2 pounds of cottage cheese) you will need:

Pasteurized skim (nonfat) milk, 1 gallon
Cultured buttermilk, $\frac{1}{2}$ cup
Heavy cream, about $\frac{1}{4}$ cup
Salt
Scallions (green onions), $\frac{1}{2}$ pound (optional)

Heatproof bowl, 6-quart; kettle, 6-quart; bowl, 3-quart; cheesecloth, 1 yard square; colander; milk pan, 8-inch

Mix milk and buttermilk in the bowl, cover, and let stand at room temperature until it smells slightly sour and has "clabbered," resembling pudding. This will take a day or two.

Fill the preserving kettle one-third full with cold tap water and place on burner. Set bowl of milk into it double-boiler style. Heat the kettle *very* gradually until puddinglike curds form with a whitish liquid, the whey, rising above it. During this time—up to an hour—the water must not boil and the milk must not be stirred.

When curds are well formed, remove bowl from heat and pour off whey into smaller bowl. Taste whey; if you prefer not to drink it, use it to fertilize the garden.

Dampen cheesecloth and line the colander with several thicknesses, placing milk pan underneath. Pour in curds and press out excess whey with large spoon. Gather up the cloth around the curds, take it to the sink, and twist to squeeze out more whey. Rinse the wrapped curds under cold water, then squeeze again.

Wash the large bowl and turn curds into it. Mash with a fork and work in just enough heavy cream to keep the curds together. Add salt to taste. Shape with spoon and palm into balls the size of oranges. Chill on a platter until serving time.

For cottage cheese balls with onions, served by Ma the hot eve of Mary's departure for college, chop the scallions and add them to the mixture before forming the balls.

HARD CHEESE

With a little improvising you can make hard cheese the way Ma did during the summer in the Big Woods of Wisconsin. The whole process will take from one morning to the next and will require some special but inexpensive materials, listed below.

Hard cheese is aged and can be mild or sharp in flavor, depending on how long you keep it before eating. Ma's cheese was stored for winter, when there was no fresh milk available. Her cheese, from grass-fed Guernsey or Jersey cows, was yellow; yours, from homogenized milk, will be white. The milk Ma used was fresh—the settled, skimmed evening milk plus whole morning milk. Yours, too, should be as fresh as possible. If you can't buy it at a dairy or dairy store, ask the supermarket manager the best time to buy fresh milk at his store. You will need both homogenized milk and cultured buttermilk to re-create Ma's summer-ripened raw milk.

Rennet, the coagulant that Ma extracted from part of a calf's stomach, can be bought in dry tablet form. Concentrated cheesemakers' rennet is a specialty item. Our recipe calls for the kind found in supermarkets and pharmacies under the brand name "Junket," not to be confused with pudding mix.

The aim in cheesemaking is to produce firm even curds that will easily shed the watery whey. Success depends on such factors as the ripeness, or acidity, of the milk, its temperature, the amount of rennet, and the timing of curd cutting. It's possible to make a good cheese on the first try with this recipe, but you can improve your chances by understanding just what you are doing. Consult your local library for any of a number of current books on home cheesemaking.

For a hard cheese of about 1½ pounds you will need:
Fresh homogenized milk, 6 quarts
Fresh cultured buttermilk, 2 cups
"Junket" rennet, 2½ tablets
Salt, 1½ tablespoons

You will also need:
An 8-quart pot of enamelware or stainless steel—anything that
    will take heat, except galvanized metal or aluminum.
A long knife that will reach to the bottom of the pan.
A thermometer ranging from 32° to 150°F for those who lack
    Ma's experience.
A slotted spoon.
A colander.
Cheesecloth, a 1-by-2-yard piece of the woven gauze, not the
    knitted fiber sometimes sold under the same name.
A drainboard, tilted and grooved like the one Pa made (can be
    plastic).
A cheese hoop and follower (the mold plus the "round board
    cut small enough to go inside the cheese hoop"). These
    can be made from a straight-sided #10 can and a piece of
    ½-inch plywood cut round on a jigsaw. You can also use
    identical half-gallon containers, provided one fits closely
    into the other. For my tests I used cheap plastic paint
    buckets; tin bread loaf pans would also work. Whatever
    mold you choose you must puncture the bottom for
    drainage. Make holes with an icepick or large nail, working
    from the inside of the container outward.
Weights. Ma used a rock to press her cheese; modern home
    cheesemakers use screw presses. With a loaf-pan follower
    ordinary 4-pound masonry bricks work well; have at least 3
    on hand. A plastic tub used as a follower can be filled with
    stones, unopened cans of food or scrap iron. Try to
    assemble weights totaling at least 10 pounds.
A 4-quart kettle to catch the whey and you're ready to go!

RIPEN THE MILK by stirring buttermilk into the milk in the 8-quart pot. Taking about 30 minutes to do it, *slowly* heat the mixture until it is wrist temperature (85°F). Turn off the heat.

"SET" THE MILK by dissolving rennet tablets in $\frac{1}{2}$ cup of cold water and stirring the solution thoroughly into the milk for 2 minutes. Leave the milk undisturbed for 30 minutes until a firm curd forms, resembling a custard. When it breaks clean from a knife inserted and turned at an angle, you are ready for the next step.

CUT THE CURD so it will release the whey. With the long knife make pan-deep strokes in one direction, then the other, to produce 1-inch-square, pan-deep bars. Cut these bars into rough cubes with sweeping, deepening motions of a slotted spoon. Be sure to reach into all parts of the kettle.

Heat the curd *slowly* (taking 30 minutes) to a temperature that is hot on the wrist (105°F). Heating too fast will toughen the outsides of the cubes and trap the whey. Stir quietly as you heat. Once the mass was warmed, Ma "let it stand while the curd separated from the whey." Do the same, letting the cubes stand with the burner off for an hour. Stir them frequently to prevent them from settling in clumps. When you stir, test a sample by chewing. If it squeaks it is firm enough to

Drain the whey. Place the colander over the 4-quart kettle and line it with a piece of cheesecloth. Pour in the curds. Taste the "thin yellowish" whey that drains out and you will see why it is usually fed to animals or poured on the garden for fertilizer! Set the whey aside for disposal.

Salt the curd by sprinkling on salt and mixing it in with clean hands. The cheese will now look something like popped corn. Let it sit 30 minutes to cool to room temperature.

Mold the curd by placing the hoop on the drainboard and lining the hoop with wet cheesecloth as smoothly as possible. Lumpy cloth makes dents in the cheese that later can harbor dirt and mold. Transfer curds to mold by handfuls, breaking up any clumps that may have formed. Smooth the surface of the cheese and the cloth over it, trimming away any excess cloth. Cover with the follower and

Press the cheese by adding weights gradually until whey oozes from the bottom. Let stand for 30 minutes, then unwrap the cheese, turn it over, wrap it smoothly, return the follower, and increase the weight on top. Turn the cheese over two or three times. Leave the cheese under at least 10 pounds of pressure overnight.

Dress the cheese in the morning by removing weights, follower, mold, and cloth and paring off any sharp edges (the green cheese Laura and Mary liked to eat). Dip the cheese in hot water, smooth over any holes with a table knife, and wipe it dry.

LET RIND FORM by storing cheese in the warmest part of the refrigerator (45°F) for 5 to 10 days, until it has developed a tough outer skin. Turn the cheese over every day and "erase" any spots of mold with a cloth dipped in vinegar water, using salt as an abrasive.

"COAT THE CHEESE" is normally the next step. Making many cheeses in succession without the benefit of refrigeration, Ma "sewed a cloth tightly around it, and rubbed the cloth all over with fresh butter. Then she put the cheese on a shelf in the pantry. Every day she wiped every cheese carefully with a wet cloth, then rubbed it all over with fresh butter once more, and laid it down on its other side." Modern cheesemakers simplify this by dipping their cheeses in paraffin. With only one cheese, you may omit any coating, provided you

CURE THE CHEESE in the refrigerator or a cool (45° to 55°F) dry place for at least 8 weeks, turning and inspecting it daily. It will then be ready to cut and serve as mild cheese. For good sharp flavor you will have to wait at least 5 months. Good luck!

POT ROAST OF OX
WITH BROWNED FLOUR GRAVY

"Charles! However did you get beef?" Ma asked, as if she could not believe it.

"Foster butchered his oxen," Pa answered. "I got there just in time. Every last bit, to bones and gristle, sold twenty-five cents a pound. But I got four pounds and here it is! Now we'll live like kings!"

Ma quickly took the paper off the meat. "I'll sear it all over well and pot-roast it," she said.

Looking at it made Laura's mouth water. She swallowed and asked, "Can you make a gravy, Ma, with water and brown flour?"

"Indeed I can," Ma smiled. "We can make this last a week, for flavoring at least, and by that time the train will surely come, won't it?"

THE LONG WINTER

In those days "pot roast" was a Yankee term; elsewhere cooks spoke of stewing and boiling tough cuts of meat. Whatever the terms, the purpose was the same: to soften tough meat and connective tissue and to extract all possible flavor from the bones.

An ox is a steer that has worked for a living. You won't find ox meat in the supermarket today, but you will find the name attached to one beef cut, the tail. Modern oxtails are probably close to what Pa bought, only fatter.

The spices used here are some of the very ones Columbus sought for use with meat four hundred years before refrigerators came into being. The "onion stuck with cloves" so often found in meat recipes carries on this tradition.

Browned flour gravy is made with flour that has been toasted. Browned flour was made in quantities and stored in the pantry. It has somewhat less thickening power than white, but it can be mixed into hot liquid without lumping and adds flavor and color to "pot liquor."

For six small servings you will need:
Oxtails, 4 pounds
Vinegar, $\frac{1}{4}$ cup homemade (page 131)
Ground allspice, $\frac{1}{8}$ teaspoon
Ground cloves, $\frac{1}{8}$ teaspoon
Pepper, $\frac{1}{8}$ teaspoon
White flour, $\frac{1}{4}$ cup unbleached all-purpose
Salt, $\frac{1}{2}$ teaspoon

Bake-oven, 4-quart; skillet, 6-inch; bowl, 1-pint

Sear the oxtails in the bake-oven without liquid over medium heat. Turn them frequently until they are brown on all sides. This will take about 15 minutes and may be a rather smoky process. Remove bake-oven from heat and slowly add 4 cups of hot tap water, vinegar, allspice, cloves, and pepper. Cover and simmer for $1\frac{1}{2}$ hours.

Meanwhile prepare browned flour by heating flour in skillet on medium heat. Stir constantly until the flour is evenly tanned, removing occasionally from heat to prevent burning. This will take 5 to 10 minutes. Let flour cool in skillet.

After oxtail meat has cooked $1\frac{1}{2}$ hours, remove the bake-oven lid, increase heat slightly so some liquid will boil away, and cook for 30 more minutes. You should now have well-cooked oxtails in about 3 cups of liquid topped by a quantity of fat, perhaps as much as a cup. You may wish to remove this fat. The quick way is by skimming; the sure way is by chilling the pot until the fat hardens into a coating that can be lifted off the broth.

To prepare gravy just before serving, add salt to pot and decant about a cup of the hot liquid into the bowl. Make a smooth paste by stirring the browned flour into the bowl. Stir this paste, in turn, into the bake-oven liquid and let it boil up for a minute or two.

Remove half the gravy to a storage jar for another meal before serving up the oxtails.

Chapter
8

Thirst Quenchers
and Treats

THE WORLD Laura entered in 1867 was a world without wrapped candy bars, canned soda pop, packaged ice cream, and frozen layer cakes. These confections so familiar to us now require a large and steady supply of sugar. White cane sugar, as we know from the "Little House" books, was still a precious item on the frontier, but changes were in the offing. In Europe, at Napoleon's urging, sugar was being extracted from sugar beets. In England and America, factories were being built that would clarify sugar by fast new methods. New machinery was making mass production of candy possible for the first time.

Out of all this came the "penny candies" that thrilled Laura in the store—the peppermint sticks, horehound drops, ribbon candies, and valentine hearts. In time, chocolate-covered candies would appear, and still later, in 1896, the first wrapped penny candy— Tootsie Roll—would make its debut.

Laura's first train ride was also her first contact with the great American novelty chewing gum. Like the Indians before them, settlers in northern woodlands chewed resin from the wounded bark of spruce trees. By the time of the Civil War, spruce gum production was a thriving industry in Maine. Soon the newly discovered paraffin was being used to make the "long sticks of white chewing gum" of the train hawker. Then came modern chicle-based gum. At the end of the century William Wrigley added clever packaging and clever promotion to make gum chewing a nationwide movement.

As the nineteenth century gave rise to penny candy it also gave rise—quite literally—to cakes as home confections. Back in the days of fireplace cookery, steamed puddings were the principal dinner sweets. Light cakes then required egg whites to rise; they were enjoyed only by those who could afford the eggs and the labor to beat them. With the spread of cookstoves and their shallow ovens came the heyday of the dessert pie, often baked in numbers, stored in a special cupboard, and reheated for serving.

As cookstoves with ovens became more popular so did the use of another cake leaven—a chemical called saleratus that reacts with the acid of sour milk or cream to produce a gas. In the 1860's, someone was clever enough to combine this saleratus, or baking soda, with a dry acid (cream of tartar) in a single "baking powder." Now cake baking was practically instantaneous; there was no long beating of eggs, no waiting for milk to sour. You could make enough batter for all your small milk pans, bake all the batches at once, and stack up the results in a single, glorious confection. Thus was the American layer cake born. With the introduction of fine cake flour at the end of the century, its triumph over the pie as dessert favorite was assured. Food essayist Kathleen Smallzried has suggested "as American as chocolate layer cake" should replace the old apple pie standard. Apple pie, after all, was common in Europe, but chocolate comes from the New World, and round layer cakes first became popular in this country.

In a survey of confections we can't overlook liquid ones. Coca-Cola, like chewing gum, has not always been so popular around the world. It was concocted as a medicine in Atlanta, Georgia, about the time Laura was setting up housekeeping as Mrs. Almanzo Wilder. Flavored soda waters, birch beer, and root beer were common before then, but if Laura had ever tasted them, she would hardly have thrilled at ginger water in the haying fields or remembered so clearly her few tastes of lemonade.

For adults, coffee (often sweetened then with molasses) was

the favorite drink and remains so today. Over a century ago world coffee prices skyrocketed when disaster struck Ceylon, the principal producer. Britons promptly switched their allegiance to tea, but Americans, unable to forget the Boston Tea Party, remained by and large a nation of coffee drinkers. Poor as they were, Ma and Pa Ingalls would not have left the Big Woods of Wisconsin without their grinder and a supply of coffee beans. How they would have enjoyed the convenience of preroasted, preground, vacuum-packed electric percolator coffee!

Unlike many pioneer families, the Ingallses seem to have imbibed little alcohol, although ale, beer, and wine were not uncommon as family drinks where milk was in short supply. Many found, in the cold of a pioneer wagon or shanty, that "an ounce of firewater in the belly is worth a pound of wool on the back." The firewater might be whiskey or a highly alcoholic medicine.

Flavors are important aspects of confections, and it is interesting to reflect on the range that Laura and Almanzo knew in their youth. As in clothing, décor, and art, there are fashions in flavors, with the rare in vogue until it becomes commonplace.

The spices of India still served much as they did in Columbus's time—to mask the tainted flavors of unrefrigerated meat, to vary the taste of pickled and salted foods, and to offset the strong flavors of animal fat and natural sweetening. Even the maple flavoring we cherish now for syrup must have been tedious to the Ingallses; its imprint on confections could be offset only by strong flavors like ginger and cloves. The wintergreen essence bottled by Mother Wilder would have had the same effect. An alcohol solution, it can still be found in drugstores, although peppermint has become a more widespread variant.

In baked goods, a bit of flavoring was usually needed to cover the "chemical" taste of baking soda and early baking powder. In Ma's day that might be rose water, made from rose petals at home, brandy, or lemon, imported from Spain before the tropical lemon found a permanent home in southern California. Gradually these and other flavors yielded to that of the vanilla bean. Today vanilla is so popular that the demand for it in ice cream production alone exceeds the world's natural supply, and the flavor must be produced artificially in the laboratory.

One unique American treat links families of today with the Ingallses and the Wilders in spite of vast changes in social customs. It is popcorn. The small-kerneled corn that bursts under heat has been hybridized in our century to produce fluffier corn and fewer duds, but the parent plants and popping go back to the first Americans. Popping corn is the chief farm product of Nebraska. Americans eat 383 million pounds of popped corn a year, mostly at home, although the ritual of popcorn eating at movies has kept many theaters from bankruptcy. Popcorn and America are indivisible. As we pioneer new frontiers in space, popcorn will probably not be far behind.

EGGNOG

In middle of the morning, Mother blew the dinner horn. Almanzo knew what that meant. He stuck his pitchfork in the ground, and went running and skipping down across the meadows to the house. Mother met him on the back porch with the milk-pail, brimming full of cold egg-nog.

The egg-nog was made of milk and cream, with plenty of eggs and sugar. Its foamy top was freckled with spices, and pieces of ice floated in it. The sides of the pail were misty with cold.

Almanzo trudged slowly toward the hayfield with the heavy pail and a dipper. He thought to himself that the pail was too full, he might spill some of the egg-nog. . . . He should do something to save it. So he set down the pail, he dipped the dipper full, and he drank. The cold egg-nog slid smoothly down his throat, and it made him cool inside. . . .

Father always maintained that a man would do more work in his twelve hours, if he had a rest and all the egg-nog he could drink, morning and afternoon.

FARMER BOY

Eggnog has a long tradition of use on festive occasions and for the sick and feeble. Recipes for both uses have always called for rum or brandy or both. Even the abstemious Shakers, according to author Caroline Piercy, used apple brandy in eggnog prepared for the sick.

Eggnog drunk in the hayfields sometimes contained hard cider. We doubt that the Wilder batch was alcoholic, for "Almanzo drank his full share" without any apparent dulling effects.

For six servings you will need:
Eggs, 6, separated
Granulated sugar, ½ cup
Homogenized milk, 1 quart
Heavy cream, 2 cups
Freshly ground nutmeg, ½ teaspoon

Bowl, ½-gallon; platter, 16-inch; milk pail and dipper or punch bowl

Beat the egg yolks and sugar in the bowl until thoroughly blended. Slowly beat in the milk, then stir in the cream. Refrigerate this mixture while you beat the egg whites on the platter until they stick to it and form soft peaks. Pour the cold egg-milk mixture into the milk pail or punch bowl and scrape the egg whites onto the surface, blending some in with a few deep strokes of the spoon. Sprinkle the nutmeg over the foamy surface and carefully dip into cups so as not to disturb the foam.

GINGER WATER

Now the sun and the wind were hotter and Laura's legs quivered while she made them trample the hay. She was glad to rest for the little times between the field and the stack. She was thirsty, then she was thirstier, and then she was so thirsty that she could think of nothing else. It seemed forever till ten o'clock when Carrie came lugging the jug half-full.

Pa told Laura to drink first but not too much. Nothing was ever so good as that cool wetness going down her throat. At the taste of it she stopped in surprise and Carrie clapped her hands and cried out, laughing, "Don't tell, Laura, don't tell till Pa tastes it!"

Ma had sent them ginger-water. She had sweetened the cool well-water with sugar, flavored it with vinegar, and put in plenty of ginger to warm their stomachs so they could drink till they were not thirsty. Ginger-water would not make them sick, as plain cold water would when they were so hot. Such a treat made that ordinary day into a special day, the first day that Laura helped in the haying.

THE LONG WINTER

Modern ginger ale has two ancestors. One is ginger beer, which was brewed and bottled at home like root beer. A fermented, bubbly drink, it was sometimes alcoholic, mostly not. The other is ginger water, or "switchel," as New Englanders called it, a non-alcoholic drink prepared for farmers during long hot days of scything in the hayfields. Modern commercial refreshers for athletes have the same thirst-quenching tartness.

Ginger comes from the root of a tropical plant. Cooks in port cities bought and used fresh ginger root in their cooking, but what reached the pioneers was usually already dried and ground to a powder.

For 6 servings you will need:
Brown sugar, $\frac{1}{2}$ to $\frac{3}{4}$ cup, packed
Powdered ginger, 1 teaspoon
Cider vinegar, $\frac{1}{2}$ cup homemade (page 131)

Jug, 2-quart, with funnel, or other half-gallon container

Dissolve brown sugar and ginger in vinegar by shaking or stirring. Add 1 quart of cold water, mix, and serve.

CAMBRIC TEA

The cold crept in from the corners of the shanty, closer and closer to the stove. Icy-cold breezes sucked and fluttered the curtains around the beds. The little shanty quivered in the storm. But the steamy smell of boiling beans was good and it seemed to make the air warmer.

At noon Ma sliced bread and filled bowls with the hot bean broth and they all ate where they were, close to the stove. They all drank cups of strong, hot tea. Ma even gave Grace a cup of cambric tea. Cambric tea was hot water and milk, with only a taste of tea in it, but little girls felt grown-up when their mothers let them drink cambric tea.

THE LONG WINTER

Tea has been a touchstone of two American revolutions. The hated tea tax that prompted the Boston Tea Party and led to the War of Independence helped make us not only a nation, but a nation of coffee drinkers. A century later, tea was the center of a bloodless revolution in grocery merchandising, when the Great American Tea Company sidestepped brokers and began selling the leaves directly from dockside cargoes to consumers. While coffee remained king, the lower price of tea did much to restore its popularity. The company became the A&P, and the change led eventually to modern supermarkets.

The tea Ma bought was from India or China and probably black, or fermented. Green tea, of dried leaves, was considered too stimulating for children.

While faraway temperance crusaders deplored cambric tea as a way of introducing stimulants to the young, the Ingallses fought the cold with a hot drink shared.

The widespread use of tea bags has made us forget how pleasant, easy, and sociable it is to brew tea in a pot. This recipe should remind us.

For six servings of tea you will need:
Black tea, 7 rounded teaspoons
Homogenized milk
Brown sugar

Teakettle, 6-cup; teapot, china or pottery, 1-quart

Fill teakettle with water and bring it to a brisk boil. Pour some in the teapot, wait a minute, then pour it out. Return kettle to boil. Put tea in pot and cover it with boiling water, until the pot is half full. Keep water in kettle hot while tea steeps in pot, at least 5 minutes.

For each serving pour a small amount of strong tea in a cup and fill up with hot water. For cambric tea half-fill the teacup with milk, add hot water until almost full, and pour in just enough tea to color. Serve tea with brown sugar for sweetening.

For delayed serving no effort need be made to keep the tea in the pot hot as long as boiling water is added to it. For second helpings hot water may be poured on the leaves.

LEMONADE

A glossy white cloth covered the table. On it was a beautiful sugar-white cake and tall glasses. . . .

"Is your lemonade sweet enough?" Mrs. Oleson asked. So Laura knew that it was lemonade in the glasses. She had never tasted anything like it. At first it was sweet, but after she ate a bit of the sugar-white off her piece of cake, the lemonade was sour. But they all answered Mrs. Oleson politely, "Yes, thank you, ma'am."

ON THE BANKS OF PLUM CREEK

Lemonade, we are told by James Trager, a collector of food facts, was invented in Paris in 1630 "following a sudden drop in the price of sugar." It remained for most Americans an exotic treat until irrigation turned barren Florida and California lands into citrus ranches and refrigerated rail cars began to distribute their produce across the country.

All citrus skins have pores through which they can lose moisture. To prevent drying, commercially grown lemons, oranges, and grapefruits are lightly waxed after being cleaned. Since this recipe uses whole lemons you will need to remove the wax at the outset by bathing the lemons in freshly boiled water. This bath, by the way, will also increase the juice yield.

For six servings you will need:
Lemons, 5 large or 6 medium
Granulated sugar, 1½ cups
Ice, crushed or cubes

Bowl, 2-quart; kitchen towel; wooden spoon or potato beetle;
   pitcher, 3-quart

Put lemons in bowl, cover with boiling water, and let stand for 2 minutes. Pour off water, wipe out bowl, and place lemons on towel. Pressing as you go, roll each one to dry it and free up juice.

Slice the lemons thin. So you do not lose any juice, either hold them over the bowl while slicing or cut on a saucer or grooved board. Place slices in bowl, sprinkling each layer with sugar until it is all used up. Let stand 25 to 30 minutes. Press well with spoon or beetle, taking care not to break up the pulp.

Put bowl contents in pitcher and fill with 3 quarts of cold water. Stir and pour into tall glasses containing ice.

PULLED CANDY

In the kitchen Eliza Jane and Royal were arguing about candy.
Royal wanted some, but Eliza Jane said that candy-pulls were only for
winter evenings. Royal said he didn't see why candy wouldn't be just
as good in the summer. Almanzo thought so, too, and he went in and
sided with Royal.

Alice said she knew how to make candy. Eliza Jane wouldn't do it,
but Alice mixed sugar and molasses and water, and boiled them; then
she poured the candy on buttered platters and set it on the porch to cool.
They rolled up their sleeves and buttered their hands, ready to pull it,
and Eliza Jane buttered her hands, too.

. . . [When the candy was cool] they all pulled candy. They pulled
it into long strands, and doubled the strands, and pulled again. Every
time they doubled it, they took a bite.

It was very sticky. . . . It should have become hard and brittle, but
it didn't. They pulled and they pulled; still it was soft and sticky. Long
past bedtime, they gave it up and went to bed.

FARMER BOY

Perhaps Eliza Jane was right after all. Candymaking is affected by air temperature and humidity, and humid summer days have spoiled many a batch.

More probably the candy stayed soft because of insufficient cooking. It is the cooking temperature of candy that determines its texture—soft, chewy, or hard. Candy thermometers, a twentieth-century invention, make it very easy to monitor boiling candy. In Almanzo's childhood the home candymaker learned to test samples in cold water for signs of various stages, called soft ball, hard ball, crack, and hard crack. A hard candy must cook longer—and get hotter—than a chewy one.

Pulling candy makes it lighter by working air into it. Young-sters who socialize today by going out for pizza or ice cream of an evening would, in Almanzo's day, have stayed home and pulled candy together.

For 1½ pounds of candy you will need:
Butter
Brown sugar, 1 cup
Light molasses, 2 cups
Vinegar, 1 tablespoon

Kettle or saucepan, 3-quart; platters, 15-inch, 2; glass, 6-ounce

Candy syrup needs room to expand when boiling, so don't skimp on pan size.

Butter the platters generously. Combine brown sugar, molasses, and vinegar with ½ cup of water and stir over high heat until boiling starts. Lower heat to medium, add a "walnut-size piece" of butter, and continue to cook, stirring frequently to prevent sticking.

After 10 minutes make the first test by dripping syrup from spoon into glass of cold water. The drops may dissolve and make the water cloudy, or they may form soft balls. Repeat drip tests every few minutes, using clean water each time. The candy is ready to remove from heat when a sample forms a hard ball in the water (250° to 260°F).

With one person holding the pot and the other scraping out the contents, pour candy on greased platters. Let candy cool about 5 minutes. Grease hands well with butter and begin to "work" it by pulling cooled edges toward the middle. When a lump is cool enough to handle pick it up, pull it with fingers to a length of about a foot, press ends together, and hold with one hand while grasping the center fold with the other. Keeping fingers well greased, repeat this as often as you can before candy stiffens. When it is cool and fairly stiff, twist into a long rope and place on a greased surface (it can be coiled on the platter). Mark with a knife for breaking into small pieces. Break up the candy when it is completely cool.

If candy fails to harden, return it to kettle with an additional ¼ cup of brown sugar. Cook. Test and repeat procedure for cooling and pulling.

MOLASSES-ON-SNOW CANDY

*Ma was busy all day long, cooking good things for Christmas.
. . . One morning she boiled molasses and sugar together until they made
a thick syrup, and Pa brought in two pans of clean, white snow from
outdoors. Laura and Mary each had a pan, and Pa and Ma showed
them how to pour the dark syrup in little streams on to the snow.*

*They made circles, and curlicues, and squiggledy things, and these
hardened at once and were candy. Laura and Mary might eat one piece
each, but the rest was saved for Christmas Day.*

LITTLE HOUSE IN THE BIG WOODS

This is a variation on maple-sugar-on-snow, a candymaking
custom that goes along with sap-boiling wherever maple sugar is
produced. In December there would have been no maple syrup to
cook to the candy stage; the sap from the previous spring's harvest
would long since have been made into sugar, which was easier to
transport and store than syrup.

For this seasonal specialty, it's helpful to have two people—
one to watch the bubbling molasses while the other readies the
pans. Don't be tempted to eat the snow, which may contain pollu-
tants.

For $\frac{3}{4}$ pound of candy you will need:
Dark molasses, 1 cup
Brown sugar, $\frac{1}{2}$ cup

9-inch pie pans, 4; saucepan with lip, 2-quart; glass, 6-ounce;
    heatproof pitcher, 1-cup

Fill pans with fresh snow, then set outside in snow to chill
when you start cooking.

Combine molasses and brown sugar in the saucepan (don't

use a smaller one; candy needs to boil up) and bring to a boil. On medium heat continue to cook, stirring frequently to prevent burning.

After 5 minutes begin testing the syrup by dripping some from a spoon into a glass of cold water. The drops may dissolve and make the water cloudy, or they may form soft balls. Using clean water each time, repeat test every few minutes until a sample forms a firm ball in the water (245°F). Remove from heat. Pour half the hot candy into the pitcher so two people can pour two portions.

Fetch pans of snow. Working rapidly, pour hot syrup onto cold surfaces. When candy has hardened break it into bite-size pieces, setting two aside for the cooks.

COMMON FAMILY PASTE FOR PIES

Pie paste is flour, fat, and water mixed in such a way that the fat particles are held in the flour without being absorbed. Rolled thin and baked, this paste produces layers of flat flakes with air between. Making good piecrust takes light handling and cool ingredients. " 'Keep cool' is a cardinal motto for pastry makers," one bygone cook wrote.

Old-fashioned homemade pie pastry is a vanishing art in fat-conscious, fast-food America. "Nothing in the whole range of cooking is more indigestible than rich piecrust . . ." sounds like a modern judgment, but it was written in Laura's youth. The idea that anything so good must be bad for you is always with us.

This recipe for one pie shell can be doubled for a covered pie. As the name suggests, it was used for everyday meat and dessert pies. For special occasions the cook worked the top crust into fine pie paste (following recipe).

Today we prebake pie shells or thicken juices to prevent soggy piecrust. Frontier cooks, as a rule, expected the bottom crust to absorb juices and greased the pie pan to prevent the wet crust from sticking.

For one 9-inch pie shell you will need:

White flour, 1¼ cups unbleached all-purpose, plus extra for
    dusting
Salt, scant ½ teaspoon
Lard, ⅓ cup (5 tablespoons)
Butter, ½ teaspoon

Bowl, 2-quart; pastry surface and rolling pin; pie pan, 9-inch

Chill all ingredients and bowl on ice or in refrigerator. Rinse
hands in cold water and dry them. Prepare a cup of ice water. In the
bowl mix flour and salt. Spoon the lard into the flour and blend with
fingers (not warm palms) until the mixture is uniformly coarse.
Continue to toss as you add 3 tablespoons of ice water. Press the
dough into a ball and chill it while you prepare the pie filling (in
summer Ma Ingalls might have set the dough bowl in a pan of cold
well water).

If your dough is a double recipe for making two crusts, divide
it with a knife and work with one half while the other half cools.

Dust pastry surface lightly with flour and flatten dough on it.
With floured rolling pin, roll the dough into a circle 2 inches wider
than the pan and ⅛ inch thick. To do this evenly and at the same time
keep dough from sticking to board, roll from the center of the
dough to the edge, giving it a slight turn after each roll.

Butter the pie pan. Transfer dough by folding it in quarters,
placing it in the pan, and unfolding. Trim with a knife around pan
edge. For an uncovered pie, pinch the crust all around the edge to
make a fluted border.

For a covered pie, roll the other dough half as you did the
first. After filling the bottom crust moisten its rim with a wet finger.
Transfer the top crust to the pie and trim edges. Pinch edges together with fingers or press with tines of a fork. Vent the top crust
by slashing it in a simple design like a pine tree or wheat sheaf.

Bake according to instructions with pie recipe.

FINE PIE PASTE

Fine pie paste, also called puff paste, is common pie paste that is buttered, folded, and rolled a number of times (three in this recipe; as many as nine times in others) to produce thin tender layers that fill up with hot air upon baking. It is the pastry of turnovers, Napoleons, and patty shells.

Pies in general and puff paste in particular came into vogue along with the home cookstove oven, making the nineteenth century the century of the pie. Pies produced in quantity for home consumption were made simply, but holidays, socials, and county fairs called for top crusts of this tricky and impressive pastry.

> *For one 9-inch pie covering you will need:*
> Butter, 6 tablespoons
> Common Family Paste for Pies (page 194)
> Filled pie shell
>
> Pastry surface and rolling pin

Divide butter in thirds and keep it cold while you prepare a dough ball of common family paste.

Roll out the dough in a rectangle roughly 5 by 15 by $\frac{1}{8}$ inch thick. Trim $\frac{1}{2}$ inch off a short side to use for patching any punctures that might occur in the dough (the crust won't be puffy if hot air escapes).

Take a third of the butter in your fingers, knead it a bit to soften, and pinch off small pieces. Cover the rectangle with these butter dots, except around the edges. Fold the short ends of the dough toward the center, overlapping them like a business letter. Press gently and fold pastry in half the other way. If pastry has broken anywhere, patch it with reserve dough by wetting the surfaces to be joined.

If the kitchen is warm and you are losing your cool, pause and chill the dough for 15 minutes. Roll it out again to a rectangle and repeat the buttering and folding operations. Chill dough again before rolling to a rectangle the third time. Once more knead the butter, dot the dough with it, and fold. Chill again.

FOR A TOP PIE CRUST, roll out the folded dough into a circle about 2 inches wider than the pan rim. See directions under Common Family Paste for Pies (previous recipe). Wet the edge of the filled bottom crust. Using rolling pin as carrier, transfer the fine pie paste to the surface of the pie. Press edges and trim; crimp with fingers or press with fork tines. Bake as directed in pie recipe.

FOR TURNOVERS, roll folded dough into rectangle 5 by 15 inches and proceed as directed in the recipe for Apple Turnovers (page 122).

VINEGAR PIE

No display of holiday pies, whether on the home table or at a fair or social, was complete without this country standard, a monument to ingenuity and resourcefulness. Sometimes called "poor man's pie," it took the place of lemon pie in areas where lemons were as precious as gold. We think it would have been made this way in both Malone and Wisconsin, using both eggs and butter, but frequently the pie was made without even these simple luxuries.

For six to eight servings you will need:
Common Family Paste for Pies (page 194)
Butter, $\frac{1}{4}$ cup
Eggs, 2
Granulated sugar, $\frac{1}{2}$ cup
Brown sugar, $\frac{1}{2}$ cup
White flour, $\frac{1}{4}$ cup unbleached all-purpose
Nutmeg, a few grindings
Vinegar, 3 tablespoons homemade (page 131)

Pie pan, 9-inch; tin cup; bowl, 1-pint; bowl, 2-quart

Prepare pie paste and line the buttered pie pan. Preheat the oven to 400°F. Melt butter in tin cup; beat eggs in small bowl.

In large bowl blend both sugars, flour, and nutmeg with fingers until no lumps remain. Stir in vinegar, eggs, butter, and 1 cup of water until well mixed. Pour into pie shell and bake at 400° for 30 minutes. Remove and cool until the filling is firm enough for cutting.

CUSTARD PIE

All around Almanzo were cakes and pies of every kind, and he was so hungry he could have eaten them all. . . .

When he began to eat pie, he wished he had eaten nothing else. He ate a piece of pumpkin pie and a piece of custard pie, and he ate almost a piece of vinegar pie. He tried a piece of mince pie, but could not finish it. He just couldn't do it. There were berry pies and cream pies and vinegar pies and raisin pies, but he could not eat any more.

FARMER BOY

A custard is a cooked, sweetened mixture of milk and eggs. Custards were very popular in the days before instant pudding, flavored gelatin, and store-bought ice cream. Plain ones were prescribed for children and invalids, while dessert custards were made in such flavors as coconut, apple, pumpkin, caramel, persimmon, and rhubarb.

Lemon rind and nutmeg were the usual flavorings for custard pies; leaves from a peach tree were also used as an accent. Modern cooks would use vanilla. With a topping of meringue or whipped cream this becomes a cream pie.

For six to eight servings you will need:
Common Family Paste for Pies (page 194)
Homogenized milk, 2 cups
Lemon rind, a quarter
Nutmeg, a few gratings
Eggs, 3
Granulated sugar, $\frac{1}{3}$ cup
Salt, a pinch
Flour, 1 tablespoon

Pie pan, 9-inch; heavy saucepan, 1-quart; bowl, 1-quart

Prepare pie paste and line buttered pie pan. Prick the paste all over with a fork to prevent bubbling, and bake it in a preheated oven at 425°F for 10 minutes. If the crust rises up despite pricking, press it down with another pie pan before it cools.

In the saucepan heat the milk just to boiling. Score and shave the lemon rind into the milk; add nutmeg.

In the bowl beat the eggs; then beat in the sugar, salt, and flour. Gradually stir in the hot milk and lemon rind mixture. Pour the custard into the saucepan and stir it over medium heat until it coats the stirring spoon with a creamy film. Pour the custard into the pie shell and bake in the oven at 425° for 10 minutes. Reduce heat to 350° and continue to bake until the filling is browned and a knife inserted comes out clean. This will take an additional 25 to 30 minutes. Serve at room temperature.

HEART-SHAPED CAKES

Those stockings weren't empty yet. Mary and Laura pulled out two small packages. They unwrapped them, and each found a little heart-shaped cake. Over their delicate brown tops was sprinkled white sugar. The sparkling grains lay like tiny drifts of snow.

The cakes were too pretty to eat. Mary and Laura just looked at them. But at last Laura turned hers over, and she nibbled a tiny nibble from underneath, where it wouldn't show. And the inside of that little cake was white!

It had been made of pure white flour, and sweetened with white sugar.

LITTLE HOUSE ON THE PRAIRIE

With so many kinds of cookies and cakes available today we can't help but be moved by the thrill Laura and Mary felt at receiving one white sugar cake apiece.

What Ma must have made, without eggs or baking powder, was something between sugar cookies and shortbread. Although there was milk on hand, we've assumed that lard, rather than butter, would have been used for baking. (You can substitute butter for lard in the ingredients below if you prefer.) We have also increased the quantity to our customary six servings and substituted a baking sheet and range oven for a bake-oven and fireplace.

For six heart-shaped cakes you will need:
White flour, 1½ cups unbleached all-purpose, plus extra for
    dusting
Granulated sugar, ⅓ cup plus extra for dusting
Baking soda, ½ teaspoon
Ground nutmeg, a pinch
Lard, ¼ cup chilled, plus extra for pan
Cultured buttermilk, ⅓ cup

Bowl, 2-quart; pastry surface and rolling pin; baking sheet; blue
    tissue paper (optional)

Preheat oven to 425°F. In the bowl mix flour, sugar, baking soda, and nutmeg. With cold fingers (dipped in cold water and dried) rub the cold lard into the dry ingredients. Make a well in the center, add buttermilk, and work with one hand into a dough that can be rolled out.

Dust rolling surface with flour. Shape the dough into a ball and roll it out into an 8-inch circle. With a table knife dipped in flour cut the circle in half, then the halves in thirds, to produce six equal wedges. Shape each wedge into a heart.

Grease baking sheet and place hearts on it so they do not touch. Bake for about 15 minutes, until cakes are puffy and nicely browned. Remove from oven and sprinkle tops immediately with sugar (the crystals will melt slightly and stick). When cool, eat or wrap with blue tissue paper, the traditional wrapping of white sugar crystals, for gift giving.

VANITY CAKES

That Saturday morning the new house was specially pretty. Jack could not come in on the scrubbed floors. The windows were shining and the pink-edged curtains were freshly crisp and white. Laura and Mary made new starry papers for the shelves, and Ma made vanity cakes.

She made them with beaten eggs and white flour. She dropped them into a kettle of sizzling fat. Each one came up bobbing, and floated till it turned itself over, lifting up its honey-brown, puffy bottom. Then it swelled underneath till it was round, and Ma lifted it out with a fork.

She put every one of those cakes in the cupboard. They were for the party.

ON THE BANKS OF PLUM CREEK

As a celebrated author, Laura Wilder was often asked how to make Vanity Cakes. In one reply, a letter now in the Detroit Public Library, she wrote, "It seems strange that I never learned to make them. I know they were mostly egg and were fried in deep fat as doughnuts are. They were to be eaten hot. Were crunchy, not sweetened and were so light, really a bubble that they seemed almost nothing in one's mouth. They were a golden color when fried. I suppose the egg yolks helped in their coloring. They simply puffed up when fried until they were nothing but a bubble: *Vanity* cakes."

Old recipes for vanities, as they are sometimes called, are deceptively simple. They don't begin to suggest the subtleties of dough texture and shape and fat temperature that make the difference between balloons and bombs, success and failure. It helps to have a lot of experience with deep-fat cooking. For those who don't, we heartily approve the use of an electric deep fryer with automatic temperature control to eliminate one of the uncertainties in making this charming and challenging confection. Our earlier caution about hot lard, page 89, applies here as well.

For six vanity cakes you will need:
Lard, 1 to 2 pounds
Egg, 1 large
Salt, a pinch
White flour, $\frac{1}{2}$ cup unbleached all-purpose
Powdered sugar, a shakerful

Deep-fat fryer or kettle, 3-quart; bowl, 1-quart; plate

Using enough lard in the fryer or kettle to produce a depth of 3 inches, heat it to 350°F. This is lower than the temperature for doughnuts.

In the bowl beat the egg and salt for a full minute. Beat in thoroughly $\frac{1}{4}$ cup of flour. Add more flour, a tablespoon at a time, until the batter is too stiff for beating but too soft to roll out.

Cover a dinner plate with flour. With a teaspoon, spoon the batter onto the plate in six separate portions. With a knife turn each spoonful of dough over to flour it, then drop it into the hot lard. Aim for a limp but compact dough mass that will not string out when it leaves the knife. If working with a mini-fryer cook no more than one at a time.

Cook each cake for at least $3\frac{1}{2}$ minutes, during which time it may need help in turning. If it darkens quickly, the fat is too hot. Drain cakes on brown paper and dust with powdered sugar.

POUND CAKE

That day they made ice-cream again, and they ate the last cake. Alice said she knew how to make a pound-cake. She said she'd make one, and then she was going to go sit in the parlor.

Almanzo thought that wouldn't be any fun. . . .

That afternoon he came into the kitchen to see if the pound cake was done. Alice was taking it out of the oven. It smelled so good that he broke a little piece off the corner. Then Alice cut a slice to hide the broken place, and then they ate two more slices with the last of the ice-cream.

FARMER BOY

Pound cake has a dense moist texture that makes it keep well and a recipe that is easy to remember—a pound each of sugar, butter, eggs, and flour. Since its arrival in America with the first English settlers it has suffered some changes. Today's plastic-wrapped store variety is a pale cousin to traditional loaves that used a glass of brandy and a full pound of butter. Alice probably skipped the brandy, but she would not have skimped on butter, a mainstay of the Wilder household. After you have made this recipe you will have great respect for her enterprise and her strength.

For a 4- to 5-pound cake you will need:
Unsalted butter, 1 pound (2 cups)
Granulated sugar, 1 pound (2 cups)
Eggs, 1 pound (8 medium)
Salt, a generous pinch
Ground nutmeg, $\frac{1}{2}$ teaspoon
Ground mace, $\frac{1}{2}$ teaspoon
White flour, 1 pound (4 cups) sifted unbleached all-purpose

Bowl, 4-quart; saucer; bowl, 2-quart; tube pan, $9\frac{1}{2}$ inches by $4\frac{1}{4}$ inches

At least an hour before starting, set out all refrigerated ingredients to warm to room temperature.

In larger bowl cream butter with wooden spoon until fluffy.
Gradually work in the sugar by pressing with spoon against bowl
side, and blend until mixture is no longer grainy. This is hard work;
it will help to work standing with the bowl at arm's length on a low
table, or sitting with the bowl in your lap.

Break an egg in the saucer. Unless it is bad, put it in the
smaller bowl (this old-fashioned two-step method keeps a bad egg
from polluting the others). Repeat for remaining eggs. Add the salt.
Beat eggs with a fork until light-colored and foamy, about *five* minutes! Add nutmeg and mace to eggs.

Stir eggs gradually into sugar-butter mixture. Sift flour and
beat in gradually, stirring only long enough to blend all ingredients.
The finished batter will be quite stiff.

Smooth the batter into the ungreased tube pan. Bake in a
preheated 350°F oven for 30 minutes, then reduce heat to 325°F and
continue to bake another 30 minutes. When a new broomstraw or
toothpick poked in the center comes out dry and the cake edges pull
away from the pan, remove pan from oven and cool. Turn cake out
and serve unfrosted.

LAURA'S WEDDING CAKE

That afternoon the finished black cashmere was carefully pressed, and then Ma made a big, white cake. Laura helped her by beating the egg whites on a platter with a fork, until Ma said they were stiff enough.

"My arm is stiffer," Laura ruefully laughed, rubbing her aching right arm.

"This cake must be just right," Ma insisted. "If you can't have a wedding party, at least you shall have a wedding dinner at home, and a wedding cake."

THESE HAPPY GOLDEN YEARS

A typical wedding cake recipe of a century ago called for "fifty eggs, five pounds sugar, five of flour, five of butter, fifteen of raisins, three of citron, ten of currants, pint brandy, fourth ounce cloves, ounce cinnamon, four of mace, four of nutmeg. This makes forty-three and a half pounds and keeps twenty years."

The groom's cake, as this was also called, was designed to provide keepsakes for wedding guests and absent friends. A slice placed under a youth's pillow was supposed to induce dreams of a future mate.

The cake actually eaten at the wedding was the "bride's cake," a white butter cake with anywhere from eight to twenty beaten egg whites. This is what Laura and Ma made.

Remember that this cake comes from the days before egg-beaters and cake flour. We ask that you beat the whites by hand not only to know what Laura felt but because the resulting texture will be different from that of machine-whipped whites.

Milk pans were the forerunners of our cake pans. Using two different sizes produces a tiered layer cake.

For a two-layer cake you will need:
Butter, 1 cup, plus 1 teaspoon for pans
Granulated sugar, 2 cups
Baking soda, $\frac{1}{2}$ teaspoon
Almond extract, $\frac{1}{2}$ teaspoon
Lemon extract, $\frac{1}{2}$ teaspoon
Homogenized milk, $1\frac{1}{3}$ cups
Egg whites, 10
Salt, a pinch
White flour, 4 cups unbleached all-purpose
Cream of tartar, 1 teaspoon

Milk pans, one 10-inch and one 8-inch, or round cake pans,
    two 9-inch; bowl, 6-quart; platter, 16-inch oval; bowl,
    2-quart

At least an hour before starting set out all ingredients to warm to room temperature. Butter pans.

In larger bowl cream butter with a wooden spoon until fluffy. Using the back of the spoon, blend in sugar until mixture is no longer grainy. This will be hard work, best done at arm's length or in the lap.

Add baking soda and almond and lemon extracts to milk and beat them into the butter-sugar blend. Place egg whites on the platter, add salt, and beat them by tracing circles in the air that catch the whites at the bottom. Beat until they are too stiff to slip when you tilt the platter. This will take about *ten* minutes. Preheat oven to 350°F.

In smaller bowl sift together flour and cream of tartar. Sift a second time. Fold flour into sugar-butter mixture a large spoonful at a time, alternating with spoonfuls of egg whites. Continue until ingredients are blended.

Divide the batter between the buttered cake pans and bake in preheated oven for 50 minutes, or until the cakes begin to pull away from the pan edges.

Cool cake layers in pans 10 minutes before turning them out on clean cloths to cool further. Meanwhile make Sugar Frosting (following recipe). Frost according to directions. Yolks from cake and frosting recipes can be used for scrambled eggs.

SUGAR FROSTING

The "sugar-white cake" of Nellie Oleson's party, the "sugar-frosted loaf of cake" for the Christmas-in-May celebration, the "white-frosted birthday cake" of Ben Woodworth's party, and Laura's wedding cake probably all had the same kind of frosting, a mixture of egg whites and powdered sugar that dries to a candylike crust. A cake fresh from a greased pan would be dusted with flour to absorb the grease, frosted once, then possibly frosted again to protect it against a dry climate.

Sugar frosting can be made without rose water, but it won't have that quaint old-fashioned flavor.

To frost two 9-inch cake layers you will need:
Egg whites, 4
Cream of tartar, $\frac{1}{2}$ teaspoon
Powdered sugar, 2 cups
Rose water, $\frac{1}{2}$ teaspoon
White flour, 2 to 3 teaspoons unbleached all-purpose

Platter, 12-inch; large fork

Beat egg whites on platter with large fork until they begin to foam. Beat in cream of tartar "to whiten and increase frothing." Add sugar a tablespoon at a time, beating after each addition, until soft peaks form and whites stick to platter. Add rose water toward the end.

Dust the slightly cooled cake with flour. Using a table knife dipped in water, spread the frosting evenly over the top and sides of one layer. Put the second layer on top and cover it with frosting. Any leftover frosting can be used for a second coating after the first has dried.

To prevent the brittle frosting from cracking while slicing, score it first with the point of the cake knife.

ICE CREAM

"Let's make ice-cream!" Royal shouted.

Eliza Jane loved ice-cream. She hesitated, and said, "Well——"

Almanzo ran after Royal to the ice-house. They dug a block of ice out of the sawdust and put it in a grain sack. They laid the sack on the back porch and pounded it with hatchets till the ice was crushed. Alice came out to watch them while she whipped egg-whites on a platter. She beat them with a fork, till they were too stiff to slip when she tilted the platter.

Eliza Jane measured milk and cream, and dipped up sugar from the barrel in the pantry. It was not common maple sugar, but white sugar bought from the store. Mother used it only when company came. Eliza Jane dipped six cupfuls, then she smoothed the sugar that was left, and you would hardly have missed any.

She made a big milk-pail full of yellow custard. They set the pail in a tub and packed the snowy crushed ice around it, with salt, and they covered it all with a blanket. Every few minutes they took off the blanket and uncovered the pail, and stirred the freezing ice-cream.

FARMER BOY

When this scene took place power-driven refrigerators and churns had not yet reached into the home, and most people bought ice cream at confectioneries and ice cream parlors. "Ice Cream Like You Buy"—the title of one old recipe—could be made in summer only by those fortunate enough to have ice as well as plenty of cream. Today "homemade" is the mark of quality ice cream, and no wonder! Compare the ingredients below with those listed on a box of supermarket ice cream (in states that require listing).

Apparently the Wilders made ice cream in staggering quantities; from our recipe you can estimate what one with six cups of sugar would produce! Nevertheless they got along without that wonderful invention of 1846, the hand-cranked portable freezer, relying instead on abundant youth-power.

For this modest amount you can substitute a two-pound coffee can, thoroughly cleaned, for the milk pail. Instead of a wooden tub, try using a one-gallon ice bucket which will allow for a 2-inch layer of ice between it and the can. A picnic cooler will also work, but the larger it is, the more ice will be needed. The salt you add to the ice will lower the freezing point and produce a solution colder than 32°F to chill the custard.

For flavoring we suggest a common one from the days before the vanilla vogue, namely, lemon. Don't expect your custard to be yellow like Eliza Jane's unless your cream comes from grass-fed Guernseys and your eggs from scratch-fed chickens.

For 1 quart of ice cream you will need:
Eggs, 3
Homogenized milk, 1 cup
Granulated sugar, 1 cup
Heavy whipping cream, 3 cups
Lemons, 2
Block ice, 5 to 7 pounds, or ice cubes, 5 to 7 trays
Coarse salt, 2 to 3 pounds

Bowl, 2-quart; platter, 12-inch; saucepan, 1-quart; coffee can, 2-pound, with lid; grain sack or pillowcase; mallet; ice bucket, 1-gallon minimum; slotted spoon; blanket or wet bath towel

Teamwork and timing are important here. The custard must be ready before the ice crushing starts. The ice team should assemble equipment in a shaded place outdoors that can't be injured by salt water.

Meanwhile in the kitchen, separate the eggs—yolks to the bowl, whites to the platter. Beat yolks about a minute, until light. Heat milk just to boiling in saucepan. Stir in sugar until dissolved. Add egg yolks. Stirring all the while, heat until mixture coats a wooden spoon with a milky film. Pour this custard in coffee can and chill (in bowl of ice or refrigerator).

Using fork, beat egg whites on platter until they are "too stiff to slip" when platter is tilted. Teamwork can accomplish this in under 10 minutes. Fold 1 cup of cream into the whites on the platter and pour the mixture into the can. Add the remaining cream and stir gently. Cover and chill 10 minutes. Squeeze lemons and strain juice to add later.

Outdoors crush ice in sack or pillowcase with mallet. Line the bottom of the ice bucket with crushed ice and salt, using three parts of ice to one of salt. Set the covered custard can in the bucket; pack sides with more ice and salt. Stop below the top of the custard can to make sure no salt enters it.

When the can is firmly packed remove the lid and stir custard with slotted spoon, scraping bottom and sides thoroughly. Stir for 5 to 10 minutes, then replace lid and cover can and cooler with blanket or wet towel. After 10 minutes repeat scraping and stirring; rest 10 minutes; then stir and scrape again. The stirring will become more difficult each time. When the custard is quite thick, stir in lemon juice and blend well.

Continue stirring and resting until the custard is too firm to move. This will take about an hour. Leave the can to chill undisturbed at least 30 minutes more. Some melting of the ice is desirable, so that subfreezing water can surround the can, but if there is no ice left, the cooler should be emptied and repacked with fresh ice and salt (or the ice cream can be removed to a freezer).

To serve, scoop into bowls with a large spoon dipped in warm water.

PARCHED CORN

> *. . . three grains of parched corn lay beside each tin plate.*
>
> *At the first Thanksgiving dinner the poor Pilgrims had had nothing to eat but three parched grains of corn. Then the Indians came and brought them turkeys, so the Pilgrims were thankful.*
>
> *Now, after they had eaten their good, big Thanksgiving dinner, Laura and Mary could eat their grains of corn and remember the Pilgrims. Parched corn was good. It crackled and crunched, and its taste was sweet and brown.*
>
> ON THE BANKS OF PLUM CREEK

Eating three kernels of parched corn is like eating only three salted peanuts—almost impossible. Let's hope that after a proper memorial to the Pilgrims, Laura and her sisters were allowed more generous helpings.

The snack shelves of supermarkets contain various fancy forms of this early American delight, but none tastier or more wholesome than the homemade thing—kernels of dried corn toasted in butter and salted. You can use Dried Corn (page 108) made from sweet corn, but the robust kernels of dried field corn are nuttier and more appealing.

For 1 cup of parched corn you will need:
Field corn, 1 ear dried, or sweet corn, 1 cup dried
Butter, 2 tablespoons
Salt

Skillet, 10-inch

If you are using field corn, shell it and remove chaff by tossing handfuls back and forth; do not wash! Heat butter in skillet over high heat. Cover the pan with kernels, reduce heat slightly, and stir constantly as kernels brown, puff up, and crackle. Cook 3 to 5 minutes. Remove from heat, salt to taste, and serve.

POPCORN

When the work was done, Father came up the cellar stairs, bringing a big pitcher of sweet cider and a panful of apples. Royal took the corn-popper and a pannikin of popcorn. . . .

They all settled down cosily by the big stove in the dining-room wall. . . . Royal opened its iron door, and with the poker he broke the charred logs into a shimmering bed of coals. He put three handfuls of popcorn into the big wire popper, and shook the popper over the coals. In a little while a kernel popped, then another, then three or four at once, and all at once furiously the hundreds of little pointed kernels exploded.

When the big dishpan was heaping full of fluffy white popcorn, Alice poured melted butter over it, and stirred and salted it. It was hot and crackling crisp, and deliciously buttery and salty, and everyone could eat all he wanted to.

FARMER BOY

When they were gone, Mrs. Boast took a full paper bag from under the dishes. "It's for a surprise," she told Laura. "Popcorn! Rob doesn't know I brought it."

They smuggled the bag into the house and hid it in the pantry, whispering to tell Ma what it was. And later, when Pa and Mrs. Boast were absorbed in checkers, quietly they heated fat in the iron kettle and poured in a handful of the shelled popcorn. . . .

Ma dipped the snowy kernels from the kettle into a milkpan, and Laura carefully salted them. They popped another kettleful, and the pan would hold no more. Then Mary and Laura and Carrie had a plateful of the crispy, crackly melting-soft corn, and Pa and Ma and Mr. and Mrs. Boast sat around the pan, eating and talking and laughing, till chore-time and suppertime and the time when Pa would play the fiddle.

BY THE SHORES OF SILVER LAKE

No plans had been made for Christmas Eve at home, so everyone had much to do. In the kitchen Laura was popping corn in the iron kettle set into a hole of the stove top from which she had removed the stove lid. She put a handful of salt into the kettle; when it was hot she put in a handful of popcorn. With a long-handled spoon she stirred it, while with the other hand she held the kettle's cover to keep the corn from flying out as it popped. When it stopped popping she dropped in another handful of corn and kept on stirring, but now she need not hold the cover, for the popped white kernels stayed on top and kept the popping kernels from jumping out of the kettle.

THESE HAPPY GOLDEN YEARS

Before the days of electric poppers there were three favorite ways of popping corn. Over live coals you used a wire popper on a long handle, placing in it only the corn. On the cookstove you would use an iron kettle with either salt or butter. Laura Wilder's accounts of all three methods suggest that they are equally good when combined with warmth, leisure, and good fellowship.

If you have never popped corn on salt, we urge you to try it. You will need salt that is coarser than the stuff in table shakers; it is sold variously as "coarse salt," "kosher salt," and "pickling salt." We like this method because it seems to leave the fewest unpopped kernels, it omits the smell of hot fat, and it eliminates pot washing.

For 6 quarts of popped corn you will need:
Coarse salt, 3 handfuls ($\frac{3}{4}$ cup)
Popping corn, 3 handfuls ($\frac{3}{4}$ cup)
Butter, $\frac{1}{4}$ pound (optional)

Kettle with lid, 5- to 6-quart; pan, 6-quart; tin cup for melting
    butter

Cover the bottom of the kettle with salt, about $\frac{1}{2}$ cup of it. Using two kernels as a test, cover and heat the kettle until they pop. Remove them, add a handful of popping corn, and cover. Return to heat until popping noise becomes intense. Remove from heat and take off cover only after popping noise stops.

Try Laura's method (of stirring, then adding more kernels while popped corn serves as cover) only if your kettle is at least 8 inches deep. Otherwise spoon the popped corn into the pan, throw away any unpopped kernels, and replenish the coarse salt. Repeat until all corn is popped. Serve in bowls with a shaker of table salt.

Or, like Almanzo's family, melt the butter in the tin cup, pour it over the full pan of corn, sprinkle with table salt, and toss lightly before serving.

POPCORN BALLS

> *Ma was boiling molasses in a pan. When Laura's kettle was full of popped corn, Ma dipped some into a large pan, poured a thin trickle of the boiling molasses over it, and then buttering her hands, she deftly squeezed handfuls of it into popcorn balls. Laura kept popping corn and Ma made it into balls until the large dishpan was heaped with their sweet crispness.*

THESE HAPPY GOLDEN YEARS

Homemade popcorn balls have gone out of style with the coming of orthodontists and braces, but they are still fun to make even if you use them only as Christmas tree ornaments. Making them is strictly a social activity, for several pairs of hands are needed to shape the balls quickly before the candy hardens.

For 2 to 2½ dozen popcorn balls you will need:
Popped corn, 6 quarts
Molasses, 2 cups
Butter, 3 to 4 tablespoons

Pan, 6-quart; baking sheets, 2; kettle, 3-quart

Spread the unsalted unbuttered corn evenly in the 6-quart pan. Butter the baking sheets lightly.

In the kettle (don't skimp on size—molasses will expand) bring molasses to a boil and cook it over medium heat, stirring frequently with a spoon. Do *not* be tempted to pour a "thin trickle of boiling molasses" over the popcorn as Ma did, for molasses that pours freely is undercooked. Yours will not be ready until it leaves the tilted pan in frothy blobs. To determine just when the molasses is ready, use the testing directions for Pulled Candy (page 190), and stop cooking when test drops of syrup harden quickly in cold water (250° to 266°F).

Spread the bubbling candy over the corn and toss quickly with the stirring spoon to distribute it. With buttered hands—four at least, six preferably—shape handfuls into balls the size of medium oranges. Place on baking sheets until cool.

If the balls are being made ahead of time for party guests or Halloweeners, store them in airtight tins or bags, so that the candy does not draw moisture and make the corn soggy.

POPCORN AND MILK

Almanzo looked at every kernel before he ate it. They were all different shapes. He had eaten thousands of handfuls of popcorn, and never found two kernels alike. Then he thought that if he had some milk, he would have popcorn and milk.

You can fill a glass full to the brim with milk, and fill another glass of the same size brim full of popcorn, and then you can put all the popcorn kernel by kernel into the milk, and the milk will not run over. You cannot do this with bread. Popcorn and milk are the only two things that will go into the same place.

Then, too, they are good to eat. But Almanzo was not very hungry, and he knew Mother would not want the milkpans disturbed. If you disturb milk when the cream is rising, the cream will not be so thick. So Almanzo ate another apple and drank cider with his popcorn and did not say anything about popcorn and milk.

FARMER BOY

The custom of eating popcorn with milk as you would breakfast cereal still belongs largely to the farming areas of the United States. City children who associate popcorn with circuses and movies are often surprised to read of Almanzo's fantasy.

Do you think it is true that "popcorn and milk are the only two things that will go into the same place"? Try testing Almanzo's theory next time you make popcorn, but start with a half-glass of milk just to play safe.

Glossary

Consult the index for terms defined elsewhere in the text.

BAKE-OVEN. Commonly called a Dutch oven. An iron kettle for fireplace baking, with a rimmed cover to hold burning coals. Modern bake-ovens have smooth covers, are often enameled, and are used both on stove burners and in ovens.

BAKING POWDER. A powder used as leavening in quick breads and cakes. The two main ingredients are baking soda and an acid substance such as cream of tartar. When moistened, they react to produce carbon dioxide, which raises the dough.

BAKING SHEET. A large flat metal rectangle, roughly 10 inches by 15 inches in size, with at least one turned-up edge, used to hold cookies and breads for oven baking.

BAKING SODA. Sodium bicarbonate, a white powder that reacts with an acid to produce carbon dioxide gas, which raises the dough. In baking, the acid is most commonly furnished by sour milk or cream of tartar.

BEETLE. A wooden or metal instrument for beating vegetable pieces or fibers to a pulp; a potato masher.

BLOODWARM. Lukewarm; close to body temperature, about 98°F. The proper temperature for activating yeast.

BRINE. Strongly salted water; also called "pickle."

BUHRGROUND. Ground between buhrstones or burrstones in a centuries-old milling process. Since modern high-speed roller milling requires that grain first be stripped of bran and germ, the term buhrground implies, by contrast, that a flour has been crushed from whole grain. Also called stoneground.

BUNG. The stopper in the hole used to drain a cask or keg. The hole itself is the bunghole.

BUTTERMILK. The liquid left after churning butter; usually somewhat acid. Cultured buttermilk is made by adding a lactic acid bacteria culture to fresh skim milk to give it a characteristic flavor and consistency. It may be used like soured milk in cooking.

BUTTER MOLD. A two-piece wooden form used for shaping butter into ornamental pieces and then ejecting the pieces for table use. Also called a butter pat.

CHOPPER AND BOWL. A heavy crescent-shaped blade of iron or steel with top-mounted handle, and a wooden bowl exactly curved to the shape of the blade to receive the blows of the chopper; used to chop food. Succeeded in our time by the straight chef's knife and the electric food processer.

COLANDER. A perforated bowl of metal or earthenware, usually footed and with handles, used for straining food.

CREAM OF TARTAR. A white crystal, crushed to a powder, acid in taste and action, made from the scrapings of wine vats. Combines with baking soda in baking powder.

CRIMP. As used here, to pinch the edge of pastry into a fixed wavy pattern, often sealing together top and bottom crusts. Crimping is usually done with the thumb and index finger.

CRUET. A small glass bottle for holding vinegar or oil at the table. Sometimes called a caster.

DECANT. To pour off gently, without disturbing sediment, as with wine and vinegar.

DOVER EGGBEATER. A metal utensil, patented by a leading manufacturer in the 1870s, with a pair of whisks that can be made to turn rapidly by the motion of a crank handle.

DREDGE. To coat with flour.

DRIPPINGS. The fat produced by meats as they are spit-roasted, oven-roasted, or pan-fried. Pork-fat drippings chilled to a semi-solid were a common substitute for butter at the table and in cooking.

DRIPPING PAN. A large shallow rectangular pan placed under a spit or oven rack to receive the drippings of roasting meat.

FLOUR, ALL-PURPOSE. A blend of the two main kinds of wheat flours—hard wheat flour, which is best for bread, and soft wheat flour, which is best for cakes. This white enriched flour works well for all kinds of home-baked products.

FLOUR, UNBLEACHED. Flour, milled from the starchy part of the wheat grain, that has been allowed to whiten from its initial yellowish color in the normal passage of time. Other flours are often whitened by bleaching agents.

FOLD IN. To mix food without releasing air bubbles, by bringing liquid from the bottom of the bowl up over the top layer in a continuous circular motion.

GIBLETS. The edible organs of fowl (chickens, ducks, turkeys, etc.)—usually the heart, liver, and gizzard (or second stomach).

GRAHAM FLOUR. Flour ground from the whole grain of wheat, as distinct from white all-purpose flour, produced after the bran and germ of the grain are first removed. It is named for Sylvester Graham, an early advocate of whole-grain cookery.

HOMOGENIZED MILK. Whole milk that has been mechanically processed to break up the fat globules, thus dispersing the cream permanently throughout the milk and increasing digestibility.

HYBRID. The offspring of male and female plants or animals of differing genus, species, or variety. Hybrids are induced by crossbreeding for the purpose of combining selected characteristics. Like the mule and hybrid corn, they are often, but not always, infertile.

LEAVEN. A substance introduced into a flour dough to promote fermentation or to produce a gas that will lighten the dough during baking. A yeast leaven works on starch to produce gas; a baking soda leaven reacts with an acid to produce gas. Also called leavening.

LYE. A strong alkaline solution obtained by soaking wood ashes and used in home soapmaking. Added to the water in which dried corn is boiled, it softens the skins for removal in the production of hominy.

MACE. A spice consisting of the dried fibrous covering of the nutmeg. It is ground to a powder for use in flavoring.

MILK PAN. A shallow round pan in which new milk was set until the cream rose to the top to be skimmed off in a thin sheet. Milk pans were metal, for easy scalding, as small as 8 inches and as large as 24 inches across, but seldom more than 4 inches deep. They have been replaced by home cream separators.

NUTMEG. The seed of a tree found in the East and West Indies and in Brazil. Dried and ground to a powder, the smooth oval nut is used as a flavoring in custards, eggnogs, and other milk dishes.

PASTEURIZED MILK. Milk that has been heated to 145°F for 30 minutes to destroy bacteria, then cooled immediately to 50°F and stored at or below that temperature. The process of pasteurization, named for Louis Pasteur, is also used to check fementation in cider, grape juice, and vinegar.

PECTIN. A substance, present in varying amounts in plant tissues, that combines with water, acid, and sugar to form a jelly.

PINT. Half a quart, equal in liquid measure to 28.9 cubic inches. A dry pint is slightly larger, measuring 33.6 cubic inches.

RIPE. Ready for action. Ripe fruit and vegetables are ready for use as food; ripe milk is sufficiently acid for cheesemaking; and ripe yeast dough is sufficiently glutinous to shape into bread.

ROOM TEMPERATURE. In Laura's day, temperature between 55° and 70°F; in modern times, temperature between 65° and 80°F.

ROSE WATER. A fragrant solution made by distilling fresh rose petals with water. Rose syrup is sweetened rose water.

SALERATUS. Potassium bicarbonate or sodium bicarbonate; baking soda.

SCALD. To heat milk to a temperature just below the boiling point. Also, to clean utensils, loosen the hair or feathers of a slaughtered animal, or loosen vegetable or fruit skins by dipping in boiling water.

SCORE. To scratch with lines; to furrow. A lemon skin that has been scored, or scratched with lines in opposing directions, will fall away in fine flakes when peeled.

SLOTTED SPOON. A large spoon, also called a cake spoon, that is perforated to release liquid or to incorporate air in the process of stirring. The same purpose is served by a flat whisk framed of heavy wire and laced with fine wire.

SPIDER. A cast-iron frying pan, originally made with long "spider legs" that held it above the coals on the hearth.

SPIT. An iron spike used for holding and turning meat being roasted before an open fire.

SPONGE. Dough that has been raised and turned into a light, porous mass by the action of yeast.

STARTER. A small portion of material containing the live microorganisms that will make vinegar, raise bread dough, or ripen milk for cheese. Vinegar mother, sour dough, and raw sour milk are natural starters.

TIN KITCHEN. A portable spit for roasting meats before a hearth fire. The spit is supported in a half-cylinder that curves away from the fire and often has a small door that can be opened to check the progress of the roast. Also called a Dutch oven, a tin baker, or a reflector.

TINWARE. Articles and utensils made of tin plate, which is thin sheet iron or steel coated with tin.

WATERGROUND. Ground between millstones turned by a waterwheel. Said of whole grains, to distinguish them from grains that are hulled and degerminated, then ground by high-speed steel rollers. See buhrground.

WHOLE WHEAT FLOUR. See Graham flour. Commercial whole wheat flour is usually finer in texture than buhrground or waterground whole wheat flour.

Metric Conversion Table

VOLUME

Liquid		Milliliters	Liters
1 teaspoon		5	.005
3 teaspoons = 1 tablespoon		15	.015
4 tablespoons = $\frac{1}{4}$ cup		59	.059
$\frac{1}{2}$ cup		118	.118
16 tablespoons = 1 cup		237	.237
2 cups = 1 pint		473	.473
2 pints = 1 quart		946	.946
4 quarts = 1 gallon		3785	3.785
Dry			
1 dry pint		550	.550

$\frac{1}{2}$ liter is about equal to 1 pint;
1 liter is about equal to 1 quart.

WEIGHT

Ounces	Pounds	Grams (to nearest hundredths)	Kilograms
.35		9.92	
.5		14.17	
.6		17.01	
1.0	.06	28.35	.03
4.0	.25	113.40	.11
8.0	.50	226.80	.23
16.0	1.00	453.59	.45
24.0	1.50	680.39	.68
32.0	2.00	907.18	.91

10 grams are about equal to $\frac{1}{3}$ ounce;
1 kilogram is about equal to 2 pounds.

LINEAR MEASURE

Inches:	$\frac{1}{2}$	1	4	8	12	16	18	20	24
Centimeters:	1.27	2.54	10.16	20.32	30.48	40.64	45.72	50.80	60.96

1 centimeter is about equal to $\frac{1}{2}$ inch;
10 centimeters are about equal to 4 inches;
1 meter, or 100 centimeters, is about equal to 40 inches, or 1 yard plus 4 inches.

TEMPERATURES

	Fahrenheit	Celsius or Centigrade (to nearest degree)
Home freezer	0°	–18°
Water freezes	32°	0°
Room temperature	68°	20°
Bloodwarm	98°	37°
Pasteurizing	145°	63°
Water boils (sea level)	212°	100°
Soft-ball syrup	234–240°	112–116°
Firm-ball syrup	244–248°	118–120°
Hard-ball syrup	250–266°	121–130°
Low oven	300–325°	149–163°
Moderate oven	350–375°	177–191°
Deep fat for frying	375–400°	191–204°
Hot oven	400–425°	204–218°

To convert Fahrenheit temperature into centigrade, subtract 32, multiply by 5, and divide by 9. (5 centigrade degrees are 9 Fahrenheit degrees.)

Bibliography

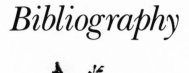

THIS LIST of books is chronological rather than alphabetical because that is the way I worked through most of them. In evaluating recipes it is helpful to know the antecedents. Valuable information also came from pamphlets on a wide variety of subjects, from apples and bacteria to salt and yeast, published by the U.S. Department of Agriculture, state wildlife departments, university extension programs, and commercial food processors.

Simmons, Amelia. *American Cookery.* 1796. Limited edition reprint. West Virginia Pulp and Paper Co., 1963.

Child, Mrs. [Lydia Maria]. *The American Frugal Housewife.* 12th ed. 1832. Reprint. [Columbus], Ohio: The Ohio State University Libraries, 1971.

Webster, Mrs. A. L. *The Improved Housewife, or Book of Receipts by a Married Lady.* 6th ed. 1845. Reprint. New York: Arno Press, 1973.

Cornelius, Mrs. [Mary Hooker]. *The Young Housekeeper's Friend.* 6th ed. Boston: Charles Tappan, 1846.

Leslie, Eliza. *Directions for Cookery, in its Various Branches.* 31st ed., 1848. Reprint. New York: Arno Press, 1973.

Hale, Mrs. [Sarah J.]. *Mrs. Hale's New Cook Book.* Philadelphia: T. B. Peterson, 1857.

Putnam, Mrs. [Elizabeth H.]. *Mrs. Putnam's Receipt Book and Young Housekeeper's Assistant.* New York: Sheldon & Co., 1867.

Beecher, Catharine, and Stowe, Harriet Beecher. *The New Housekeeper's Manual: Embracing a New Revised Edition of The American Woman's Home.* New York: J. B. Ford and Co., 1873.

Ladies of the First Presbyterian Church, Dayton, Ohio. *Presbyterian Cook Book.*
    1875. Reprint in *Midwestern Home Cookery.* New York: Arno Press, 1973.

Asher & Adams. *Asher & Adams' New Columbian Railroad Atlas and Pictorial Album of
    American Industry.* 1876. Reprint. New York: Ridge Press, Inc., Rutledge
    Books, 1976.

Tyree, Marion Cabell, ed. *Housekeeping in Old Virginia.* 1879. Reprint. Louisville,
    Ky.: Favorite Recipes Press, 1965.

Parloa, Marie. *Miss Parloa's New Cook Book.* 1880. Reprint. Minneapolis, Minn.:
    General Mills, Inc., 1974.

Chicago *Daily Tribune*, "The Home" Department. *The Home Guide; A Book by 500
    Ladies Embracing about 1,000 Recipes and Hints.* 10th ed. Elgin, Ill.: S. L. Taylor,
    1881.

Harland, Marion. *Common Sense in the Household. A Manual of Practical Housewifery.*
    Rev. ed. New York: Charles Scribner's Sons, 1881.

Practical Housekeeping. A Careful Compilation of Tried and Approved Recipes. 5th ed.
    Minneapolis, Minn.: Buckeye Publishing Co., 1885.

Cushing, Mrs. C. H., and Gray, Mrs. B. *The Kansas Home Cook-Book.* 5th ed. 1886.
    Reprint. New York: Arno Press, 1973.

Chapter 14, "St. Thecla," Christ Church, East Orange, N.J. *The Home Cook Book.*
    Orange, N.J.: Christ Church Furnishing Fund, 1889.

Gill, J. Thompson. *The Complete Practical Confectioner, in Eight Parts.* 5th ed. Chi-
    cago: Confectioner & Baker Publishing Co., 1890.

Gregory's National Cookbook. Marblehead, Mass.: James J. H. Gregory & Son,
    [n.d., about 1890].

Farmer, Fannie Merritt. *The Boston Cooking-School Cook Book.* 1896. Reprint. New
    York: New American Library, 1974.

[Ladies of Malone and others.] *The Malone Cook Book.* 3rd ed. Malone, N.Y.:
    Women's Aid Society of the First Congregational Church, 1898.

[Women's Guild of Grace Church, Madison, Wisc.] *Capital City Cook Book.* 3rd ed.
    1906. Reprint in *Midwestern Home Cookery.* New York: Arno Press, 1973.

Ziemann, Hugo, and Gilette, Mrs. F. L. *The White House Cook Book.* New and
    enlarged ed. New York and Akron, Ohio: Saalfield Publishing Co., 1909.

[Women of the Church of the Brethren.] *The Inglenook Cook Book.* 1911. Reprint.
    New York: Pyramid Publications, 1974.

Allen, Ida Bailey. *Ida Bailey Allen's Modern Cook Book.* Garden City, N.Y.: Garden
    City Publishing Co., 1924.

Medsger, Oliver Perry. *Edible Wild Plants.* New York: The Macmillan Company,
    1939.

Wolcott, Imogene. *The New England Yankee Cookbook.* 1939. Reprint. Louisville,
    Ky.: Favorite Recipes Press, n.d.

Giles, Dorothy. *Singing Valleys: The Story of Corn.* New York: Random House, Inc.,
    1940.

Rombauer, Irma S. *The Joy of Cooking.* 6th ed. Indianapolis, Ind.: The Bobbs-Merrill Company, Inc., 1946.

Berolzheimer, Ruth, ed. *Culinary Arts Institute Encyclopaedic Cookbook.* Chicago: Consolidated Book Publishers, Culinary Arts Institute, 1950.

Storck, John, and Teague, Walter Dorwin. *Flour for Man's Bread: A History of Milling.* Minneapolis: University of Minnesota Press, 1952.

Ashbrook, Frank G. *Butchering, Processing & Preservation of Meat.* Princeton, N.J.: D. Van Nostrand Company, Inc., 1955.

Keller, Allan. *Grandma's Cooking.* New York: Gramercy Publishing Co., 1955.

Smallzried, Kathleen Ann. *The Everlasting Pleasure.* New York: Appleton-Century-Crofts, 1956.

[Pioneers of the Cariboo and B.C.] *Buckskin Cookery: The Pioneer Section; The Hunting Section.* 2 vols. Quesnel, British Columbia: Gwen Lewis, 1957.

Piercy, Caroline B. *The Shaker Cookbook: Not by Bread Alone.* New York: Crown Publishers, Inc., 1958.

Burns, Paul C., and Hines, Ruth. *To Be a Pioneer.* New York and Nashville: Abingdon Press, 1962.

Gibbons, Euell. *Stalking the Wild Asparagus.* New York: David McKay Co., Inc., 1962.

U.S. Department of Agriculture. *After a Hundred Years: The Yearbook of Agriculture 1962.* Washington, D.C.: U.S. Government Printing Office, 1962.

Aresty, Esther B. *The Delectable Past.* New York: Simon and Schuster, Inc., 1964.

Editors of *American Heritage. The American Heritage Cookbook and Illustrated History of American Eating & Drinking.* [New York:] American Heritage Publishing Co., 1964.

Adamson, Helen Lyon. *Grandmother in the Kitchen.* New York: Crown Publishers, Inc. 1965.

Carson, Gerald. *The Old Country Store.* New York: E. P. Dutton & Co., Inc., 1965.

Anderson, William. *The Story of the Ingalls.* Flint, Mich: William Anderson, 1967.

Ballock, Helen Duprey, ed. *Recipes of the Westward Empire.* (Vol. 4 of *A National Treasury of Cookery* by Mary and Vincent Price.) New York: Heirloom Publishing Co., 1967.

Ballock, Helen Duprey, ed. *Recipes of Victorian America.* (Vol. 5 of *A National Treasury of Cookery* by Mary and Vincent Price.) New York: Heirloom Publishing Co., 1967.

Dickinson, Maude. *When Meals Were Meals: Recipes and Recollections from a Farmhouse Kitchen.* New York: Thomas Y. Crowell Company, 1967.

Harrison, S. G., Masefield, G. B., and Wallis, Michael. *The Oxford Book of Food Plants.* London: Oxford University Press, Inc., 1969.

Angier, Bradford. *Food-from-the-Woods Cooking.* New York: The Macmillan Company, Collier Books, 1970.

Trager, James. *The Enriched, Fortified, Concentrated, Country-Fresh, Lip-Smacking, Finger-Licking, International, Unexpurgated Foodbook.* New York: Grossman Publishers, Inc., 1970.

[Carter, Kate B., ed.] *The Pioneer Cook Book.* 4th ed. Salt Lake City: Daughters of Utah Pioneers, 1971.

Meyer, Carolyn. *The Bread Book: All About Bread and How to Make It.* New York: Harcourt Brace Jovanovich, Inc., 1971.

Beard, James A. *James Beard's American Cookery.* Boston: Little, Brown and Company, 1972.

Dworkin, Floss and Stan. *Bake Your Own Bread and Be Healthier.* New York: Holt, Rinehart and Winston, Inc., 1972.

Harris, Gertrude. *Manna: Foods of the Frontier.* San Francisco: 101 Productions, 1972.

Lowenstein, Eleanor. *Bibliography of American Cookery Books, 1742–1860.* Rev. ed. New York: Corner Book Shop, 1972.

Oddo, Sandra. *Home Made: An Alternative to Supermarket Living.* New York: Atheneum Publishers, 1972.

Smith, Dorothy. *The Wilder Family Story.* Malone, N.Y.: Franklin County Historical and Museum Society, 1972.

Alth, Max. *Making Your Own Cheese and Yogurt.* New York: Funk & Wagnalls Co., 1973.

Bruce, Jones, Briggs, and Mayer. *The Plimoth Colony Cook Book.* 4th ed. Plymouth, Mass.: Plymouth Antiquarian Society, 1973.

Gilmore, Grant and Holly. *The Homestead Kitchen and Cellar.* New York: Lancer Books, 1973.

Herman, Judith, and Herman, Marguerite Shalett. *The Cornucopia, Being a Kitchen Entertainment and Cookbook.* New York: Harper & Row, Publishers, 1973.

Lifshey, Earl. *The Housewares Story.* Chicago: National Housewares Manufacturers Association, 1973.

Graber, Kay, ed. *Nebraska Pioneer Cookbook.* Lincoln, Neb.: University of Nebraska Press, 1974.

Gregory, Mark. *The Good Earth Almanac: Old-Time Recipes.* New York: Sheed & Ward, Inc., 1974.

O'Connor, Hyla. *The Early American Cookbook.* Englewood Cliffs, N.J.: Prentice-Hall, Inc., 1974.

Anderson, Jean. *Recipes from America's Restored Villages.* Garden City, N.Y.: Doubleday & Company, Inc., 1975.

Dewey, Mariel. *12 Months Harvest.* San Francisco: Chevron Chemical Co., Ortho Books, 1975.

Editors of *Better Homes and Gardens. Better Homes and Gardens Heritage Cook Book.* [Des Moines, Iowa:] Meredith Corporation, 1975.

Hilton, Suzanne. *The Way It Was—1876.* Philadelphia: The Westminster Press, 1975.

Kreidberg, Marjorie. *Food on the Frontier: Minnesota Cooking from 1850 to 1900, with Selected Recipes.* St. Paul, Minn.: Minnesota Historical Society, 1975.

Overstreet, Daphne. *Arizona Territory Cook Book, 1864–1912.* Globe, Ariz.: Pimeria Press, 1975.

Smith, Page, and Daniel, Charles. *The Chicken Book.* Boston: Little, Brown and Company, 1975.

Stratton, Eula Mae. *The Ozarks Mountaineer Pioneer Cookbook.* 2nd ed. Branson, Mo.: The Ozarks Mountaineer, 1975.

Anderson, William T. *Laura's Rose: The Story of Rose Wilder Lane.* Mansfield, Mo.: The Laura Ingalls Wilder—Rose Wilder Lane Home Association, 1976.

Bobrowski, Robert. *Rediscovering the Woodburning Cookstove.* Old Greenwich, Conn.: The Chatham Press, Inc., 1976.

Emery, Carla. *The Old Fashioned Recipe Book, an Encyclopedia of Country Living.* 7th ed. Kendrick, Idaho: Carla Emery, 1976.

Hull, LaVerne Keettel. *Corn Country Cooking, Souvenir of Iowa.* [No publisher or date.]

[Ladies of Malone and Others.] *The Malone Cook Book.* 8th ed. Malone, N.Y.: Women's Fellowship of the First Congregational Church, 1976.

Latham, Roger M. *Complete Book of the Wild Turkey.* Harrisburg, Pa.: Stackpole Books, 1976.

Miller, Dwight, and Rogers, Suzanne D., eds. *Our Rural Heritage: A Collection of Essays and Recipes.* West Branch, Iowa: West Branch Heritage Foundation, 1976.

Nickey, Louise K. *Cookery of the Prairie Homesteader.* Beaverton, Ore.: The Touchstone Press, 1976.

Penner, Lucille Recht. *The Colonial Cookbook.* New York: Hastings House Publishers, Inc., 1976.

Seymour, John. The Guide to Self-Sufficiency. New York: Popular Mechanics Books, 1976.

Stratton, Eula Mae. *Ozarks Cookery: A Collection of Pioneer Recipes.* Branson, Mo.: The Ozarks Mountaineer, 1976.

Weymouth, Lally. *America in 1876: The Way We Were.* New York: Random House, Inc., Vintage Books, 1976.

Zochert, Donald. *Laura: The Life of Laura Ingalls Wilder.* Chicago: Henry Regnery Company, 1976.

David, Elizabeth. *English Bread and Yeast Cookery.* London: Allen Lane, 1977.

Perl, Lila. *Hunter's Stew and Hangtown Fry: What Pioneer America Ate and Why.* New York: Seabury Press, Inc., 1977.

Kurtis, Wilma, and Gold, Anita. *Prairie Recipes and Kitchen Antiques.* Des Moines, Iowa: Wallace-Homestead Book Co., 1978.

Fruit and Vegetable Facts and Pointers: A Series of Reports on Each of 78 Commodities. Washington, D.C.: United Fresh Fruit and Vegetable Association, variously dated.

Index

(Numbers in **boldface** refer to recipes.)